Free Bonus from Captivating History
(Available f ~~ Limited time)

Hi History Lovers!

Now you have a chance to jo   u can get
your first history ebook for free as well as discounts and a potential to get
more history books for free!

Simply visit the link below to join.	Or, Scan the QR code!

captivatinghistory.com/ebook

Also, make sure to follow us on Facebook, X, and YouTube by
searching for Captivating History.

Table of Contents

History of Pirates

*A Captivating Guide to the Golden Age of
Piracy and the Infamous Pirates Who
Ruled the Seas*

Introduction

Piracy is the act of robbery or criminal violence at sea. This term is rather all-encompassing. It covers a wide range of illicit activities committed at sea without the authorization of any state. Piracy usually involves attacking ships or coastal areas to steal valuables from the wealthy to sell or melt into raw materials. Historically, piracy has been viewed as a severe crime against international law. This idea has led to a universal principle that any nation can pursue and punish pirates. It didn't matter where they came from or where the crime occurred, and it still doesn't.

The history of pirates is a rich and tumultuous journey from ancient times well into our modern era. To understand where pirates came from, we need to understand the socioeconomic and political conditions that created the concept of piracy. Pirates have influenced global trade, maritime law, and even popular culture. We will explore notorious figures and the legendary exploits of pirates, but we will also analyze how much pirates impacted the world around us.

The history of pirates spans millennia, and their activities touch almost every corner of the globe. We will explore how piracy developed in ancient civilizations like the Greeks, Romans, and Phoenicians. When we think of pirates, we think of the traditional seventeenth and eighteenth-century marauders with their masted sailing ships and their feathered broad-brimmed hats, but what about the Viking raiders during the medieval era? These Norse and Dane people wreaked havoc all over Europe and into the Mediterranean. There's a reason that medieval maritime laws were designed to curb piracy. The discovery of the Americas and European expansion also had a profound effect on piracy. But what was it?

We can't talk about the history of pirates without spending a considerable amount of time on the Golden Age of Piracy. This era is where we find the most famous pirates in history and islands dedicated as pirate havens. By this point, pirates had developed their own identity using specific types of ships and weaponry. They created their own culture, with social structures and mythologies different from the rest of civilization. Women even found a place within the world of pirates.

This golden age was the peak of piracy's history, but piracy didn't disappear. While piracy never gained the notoriety it held during its golden age, the Mediterranean Sea and the seas around Asia continue to experience piracy in different cultural and political contexts. Contemporary piracy encompasses a different community and culture than it did in the past. How we view pirates is significantly affected by historical contexts and how they've been romanticized and depicted in literature, film, and the media. Pirates today do not fit this image at all.

This book is designed to offer you valuable insights into human behavior, the development of maritime law, and the dynamics of power and economic disparity. Pirates are portrayed as outlaws and rebels. They are the people who stood up against the established order and highlighted the vulnerabilities of even the most powerful empires. Journey with us as we explore piracy in the storied past and walk through the evolution of pirates and piracy's enduring legacy in the modern world.

Chapter 1 – Early Beginnings

When we hear the word pirate, we usually imagine high-seas adventure and lawless marauders. But the story of piracy stretches back much further than that. Piracy enters written history in the ancient maritime civilizations of the Greeks, Romans, and Phoenicians. These pirates aren't anywhere near the romanticized figures of more modern legend but are more practical opportunists and seafarers who turned to piracy out of need or growing ambition. In fact, the term "piracy" is traced back to the Greek word *peiráomai,* which means "attempt to steal." Over time, as the views on piracy shifted, the term changed to something similar that meant "brigand." Eventually, it became the Latin *pirata.*

Ancient Greeks

Ancient Greece was heavily dependent on a maritime culture. Piracy was more widespread, accepted, and expected. It was often viewed as a profession and a way to gain wealth and glory during the Bronze Age. Some of the first references to piracy are found in works of classical literature like Homer's *Iliad* and *Odyssey.* In Homer's tales, piracy is not only depicted as common but an honorable endeavor. Odysseus himself speaks of the many raids and acts of plundering he participated in.

Greek pirates targeted the many coastal cities and, of course, ships. The political landscape of this time was fragmented, with small kingdoms that lacked a significant naval power of their own. The pirates took advantage of this weakness. The islands of Taphos were known for inhabitants who took to the sea and often served as pirates. Again, in the

Odyssey, Penelope rebukes suitors by mentioning the Taphian sea robbers.

Things changed as Greek city-states started to consolidate power and unite. The need for income to support these new governments meant a growing interest in protecting the exchange of goods. Part of this endeavor was combating piracy. These new states began to create their own naval forces that patrolled the seas more effectively, making piracy that much more difficult. As a result, piratical activities lessened. For example, the Athenian General Cimon is said to have driven the Dolopian pirates out of the Aegean island of Scyros sometime around 475 BCE.

The creation of powerful city-states like Athens did not eliminate piracy, though. Piracy continued throughout the Hellenistic period. When Alexander the Great died, there was a major comeback for pirates. In the chaos after his death, the area was flooded with independent brigands and state-hired mercenaries turning to piracy to make ends meet. Thucydides (a Greek historian) noted that previously, piracy was considered an acceptable livelihood and held prestige. His choice of words implies that, by this time, the view of pirates and piracy had changed to something more criminal.

Piracy was a tool of political power as well as a means for collecting personal riches in ancient Greece. Polycrates, the ruler of Samos, was considered a tyrant during this period. He used his impressive naval powers to conduct raids and gained notoriety through his exploits, including raiding other city-states. He grew a considerable amount of wealth through these piratical activities.

Famous Greek Pirates

Dionysius the Phocaean

Dionysius was not only a pirate but also an admiral during the Persian Wars (fifth century BCE). He failed miserably during the Battle of Lade in 494 BCE and decided to turn to piracy as a new professional endeavor. He successfully attacked trading vessels and moved his operations to Sicily where he could target the wealthy Carthaginian and Tyrsenian (Tyrrhenian) merchant ships. He remained loyal to Phocaea and Greece and refused to attack Greek vessels.

Glaucetas

Ancient Greek inscriptions mention this Greek privateer, also known as Glauketas, who was active in piracy over the Aegean Sea during the fourth century BCE. The Athenian Navy, under the command of Thymochares of Sphettos, raided Glaucetas' base on Kythnos, where they captured him and his men.

Panares

Panares was a general of the ancient Cretan city of Kydonia, labelled as a pirate home. In 69 BCE, the Romans attacked it in their effort to fight piracy. Panares surrendered to Marcus Antonius, marking a Roman victory in the fight against piracy.

Ameinias the Phocian

Known as a Greek pirate and mercenary leader, Ameinias served King Antigonus II Gonatas of Macedon in the third century BCE. Ameinias began as a pirate captain. Later in life, he was employed by Antigonus to take down the "tyrant" Apollodorus of Cassandreia. He was successful and continued to serve Antigonus. This famous pirate is another example of how fluid the boundaries were between piracy and mercenary activities in ancient Greece.

Dionysius of Syracuse

Also known as Dionysius I, he was a tyrant ruler during the late fifth century and early fourth century BCE. He was known best as a political and military leader. His aggressive naval policies and frequent use of mercenaries got him labeled as a pirate. He used his fleet to control trade routes and raid enemy territories.

Romans

The Romans were constantly at war with the Cilician pirates who operated along the southern coast of what is now Turkey. Cilician pirates were notorious for their fast and agile ships (lembi) that could navigate these coastal waters with ease but also evade larger naval vessels. These pirates were successful enough that they kidnapped famous figures.

These pirates posed a serious threat to the Roman maritime trade empire. They target the slower-moving grain ships that were important to the empire's food supply. The crews of the ships were captured and sold as slaves, while the elite were held for ransom. The slave trade during this era was quite lucrative and only served to fuel the pirates' activities.

They were one of the fiercest destabilizing forces in the Mediterranean.

One of the most famous incidents with these particular pirates was their capture of Julius Caesar. In 75 BCE, a young Caesar was traveling to study in Rhodes when he was seized by pirates. Plutarch wrote that he displayed a remarkable audacity toward his captors. Caesar demanded that the pirates increase the ransom they were asking for to have him returned since he didn't believe their first price equaled his worth. The ransom was paid, and Caesar was released. After his release, he vowed to punish the pirates. He eventually captured and crucified all the pirates who had kidnapped him, fulfilling his promise.

A few years later, the pirate problem was still growing. Rome granted Pompey the Great a set of tremendous powers through the Gabinian law in 67 BCE. He launched a campaign against the pirates that proved to be quite effective. Logistically, he divided the Mediterranean into several zones. Each of these zones was then assigned to a fleet so they could systematically clear the seas of pirates. This effort culminated in the Battle of Korakesion near modern-day Alanya, Turkey. Pompey defeated the Cilician pirates and restored safety to the Mediterranean trade routes, significantly benefiting Roman commerce.

The success of Pompey's campaign not only eradicated the immediate threat but also extended Roman influence into Asia, solidifying Pompey's position as one of the most powerful men in Rome for nearly two decades.

Phoenicians

The Phoenicians were well known as master mariners and traders, but they also dabbled in piracy when it suited them. The Phoenicians lived along the narrow coastal strip of the Levant. There, they established a vast network of trade routes across the Mediterranean. The Phoenicians had several colonies and outposts, such as Carthage. These colonies gave them safe havens as well as launching points for their raids. They were secure bases from which they could operate with relative impunity. The dual role of these outposts underscores the Phoenician's ability to adapt and thrive in both legitimate and illicit maritime ventures.

Their reputation as expert sailors was well earned. Their shipbuilding capabilities were above that of most civilizations at the time. They constructed vessels that were capable of long voyages as well as rapid maneuvers—essential aspects for both trading and piratical raids. Taking advantage of their superior seamanship and the agility of their ships, the Phoenicians targeted Greek and Roman ships most often.

The Phoenicians were rather pragmatic in their approach to piracy. They used piracy as a strategic tool to weaken their competitors or secure resources they found valuable at the time. They turned to piracy when it served their broader economic or political objectives. For instance, during times of conflict or economic downturn, they could easily switch from legitimate trade to piracy.

Why Turn to Piracy?

The rise of piracy in the ancient Mediterranean was driven by a complex combination of economic, social, and political factors. All these worked together to create an environment where piracy could not only thrive as a livelihood but also served as a strategic tool.

Economic disparities were a large contributor to the rise of piracy. Many of the coastal regions, like Cilicia in Asia Minor, were economically disadvantaged. The rough terrain there made agriculture challenging. This pushed local fishermen and small-scale traders toward piracy because it was a far more lucrative alternative. The dream of wealth and a better life was a powerful motivator for many to join pirate crews.

Many of these societies also had rigid class structures, so the social mobility piracy offered was appealing to individuals who were trapped in lower socioeconomic classes within these civilizations.

Combine these disparities with the presence of an extensive trade network, and you have the perfect environment for piracy. The ancient trade routes connected wealthy cities and empires, including those of the Greeks, Romans, and Phoenicians. Merchant trips were frequent targets as they crossed the Mediterranean. These ships carried valuable cargo loads ranging from grain and olive oil to luxury goods and even slaves and were highly attractive to pirates. What's more, all the Mediterranean's little islands and hidden coves created ideal hiding spots for pirate ships to sit and wait to ambush or evade capture.

Lastly, political instability pushed piracy to its peak. This era experienced extensive periods of war and civil strife. With the conflicts that followed the death of Alexander Great and the Roman civil wars, naval powers had to divert their resources from protecting trade routes to engaging in military campaigns. Pirates took advantage of this diversion.

At the same time, some of these states tacitly or even overtly supported piracy to weaken their enemies or gain economic advantages for themselves. During the Hellenistic period, pirates were employed as mercenaries by warring states, which only blurred the lines further between piracy and state-sanctioned privateering.

Chapter 2 – The Medieval Era

The appeal of piracy was too great for Pompey's campaign against them to last long. After the fall of the western Roman Empire, piracy in the Mediterranean continued but adapted to new political realities. The decline of centralized Roman control and the fragmentation of political power across Europe created fertile ground for pirates to thrive.

Yet again, piracy was often intertwined with political and military strategies during the early medieval period. Byzantine emperors occasionally employed pirates as mercenaries against their rivals. A variety of new pirate activity also evolved. This included the raiding Norse Vikings in northern Europe and the Mediterranean corsairs.

Viking Raiders

The Viking age spanned from the late eighth century to the early eleventh century. While many believe that Viking is the name for a culture, it's actually the name for an activity. Norsemen from Scandinavia (modern-day Norway, Sweden, and Denmark) went raiding, or "viking." Viking raids profoundly shaped the political, social, and economic landscapes of Europe, in particular the British Isles and Frankish territories.

Raids and Methods

The beginning of the Viking age was marked by the infamous attack on the Lindisfarne monastery in 793 CE. This was the first account of a Viking attack. The raid was ferocious and went down in history as a barbaric and violent attack on Christianity—on innocent people. This particular raid set a precedent for the ferocity and strategic brilliance of Viking raids. The Vikings targeted monasteries, coastal villages, and trading ports across Europe because they knew they held the most wealth and had relatively poor defenses. Norsemen constructed fast and agile longships, which were the key to their success. Their vessels could navigate both open seas and shallow rivers, which allowed them to swiftly strike anywhere and retreat with their plunder at an equally fast rate.

Unlike regular piracy, Viking raids were seasonal. They were often conducted during the summer when the weather conditions were favorable for sailing. Their raids were small-scale and only involved a few ships. Over time, however, they grew in scale and organization. The Great Heathen Army invaded England in 865 CE. This was a notable example of a large and well-coordinated fighting force that wreaked havoc across the lands.

Motivations

Much like most pirates, the search for wealth was a primary driver for Viking raids. The riches they pillaged from monasteries and towns included gold, silver, and other valuable goods.

Scandinavia was also experiencing significant population pressures at this time. Their population was growing, yet the arable land was limited. This was especially so in regions like Norway. Raids were conducted not only to gain wealth for the lords but also to discover new land for settlements. New and highly arable land in places like England offered them a solution to these issues. They conquered and found new territories for cultivation and habitation. So, piracy turned into colonization.

Norse and Dane society valued bravery and military prowess, and how they performed on the battlefield said a lot about them. A successful raid elevated the status of the warriors and leaders involved. Raids provided them with not only wealth but also prestige within society. Their societal structure even encouraged young men (and, evidence shows, young women as well) to join raiding parties in pursuit of honor as well as material gain.

Impacts of Viking Pirates

The style of these Viking pirates often led to political upheaval in the areas they raided. As England was their target for quite some time, the establishment of the Danelaw on English soil was a direct result of the Viking raids and Viking piracy. This was a Scandinavian colony in Great

Britain set aside for Norse and Dane settlements. This region saw a fusion of Norse and Anglo-Saxon cultures and had a huge role in the development of English society.

The Viking raids helped facilitate cultural exchange between Scandinavia and the wider European world. Norse traders and settlers went to these areas and introduced new technologies, crafts, and cultural practices. The integration of Norse elements into the local culture resulted in changes to place names, legal practices, and even languages.

The Vikings presented a persistent threat to other European civilizations. This forced the development of new military strategies and types of fortifications. The coastal communities and the monasteries very quickly improved their defenses. The larger political entities, like the kingdoms of England and Francia, reorganized their military structures specifically to counter the Viking threat.

The raiding bases that the Vikings established in Normandy, Ireland, and Russia eventually became permanent settlements—thriving communities that began to play a significant role in regional politics and trade.

Arab Pirates in the Mediterranean

The early medieval period witnessed the rise of corsairs, or Arab pirates, who posed a significant threat specifically to Christian shipping in coastal towns across the Mediterranean. The corsairs operated primarily from bases in North Africa and the Levant. They very easily exploited the political fragmentation and rich economic opportunities in the region and became formidable adversaries.

One of the most notorious havens established by these Arab pirates was the Emirate of Crete, founded in the ninth century. It became a central base for launching raids across the Aegean Sea, targeting Byzantine territories. These pirates caused significant disruption to trade and local economies since Crete sat at a very strategic location that allowed the corsairs to control key maritime routes. They could strike at both mainland Greece and the surrounding islands with intense freedom.

The Byzantine Empire tried repeatedly to reclaim Crete but didn't succeed until Nikephoros Phokas' campaign in 961 CE. This success significantly curtailed the activities of the corsairs in the region, at least temporarily.

Tactics and Impacts

The corsairs used a variety of tactics that maximized their impact. Like most pirates, they used fast, agile ships that could easily outrun the heavier Byzantine vessels. This allowed them to conduct quick raids and escape before any significant military response was put together. These raids were highly successful, providing them with significant plunder that included gold, silver, and slaves. The slaves were taken back to North Africa and sold in the bustling markets there.

Their presence in the Mediterranean had weighty economic and social impacts. The coastal communities lived in constant fear of raids. They fortified their towns and developed better defensive measures in response. Both Byzantine and later European naval powers had to invest heavily in their maritime defenses and fleets to gain even the tiniest bit of advantage over the pirates.

Political and Military Involvement

The decline of the Byzantine Empire's naval power with the subsequent rise of competing Islamic states in North Africa provided a fertile ground for piracy. The lack of a strong and decentralized naval force allowed pirate groups to operate with relative freedom. The local rulers often supported or simply tolerated the pirates because they benefited from the economic boost provided by their activities.

The corsairs, like their predecessors, were often integrated into larger geopolitical conflicts. Many of the Muslim states employed the pirates during wars against Christian powers. Yet again, a blending of piracy and state-sponsored privateering further complicated any efforts being made to eradicate piracy and its influence.

The Catalan and Aragonese

The Crown of Aragon, which included Catalonia, was an impressive maritime power in the Mediterranean during the medieval period. The Catalan naval power expanded, taking aggressive action against both Muslim and Christian states. This contributed heavily to the volatile maritime environment of the era.

The Catalan territories, particularly Barcelona, Mallorca, and Valencia, were deeply involved in maritime trade from the twelfth to the fifteenth centuries. Their commercial activities extended from the regions of Occitania and France as far as the Mediterranean Levant and the Atlantic territories. The Catalan merchants traded a variety of goods that included saffron, dried fruits, wool, ceramics, and glass items. The extensive nature of this trade network required a strong naval presence for protection and often more aggressive maritime strategies to safeguard their interests and expand their influence.

One of the most noteworthy entities of the Catalan maritime scene was the Catalan Company. This company was a group of mercenaries led by Roger de Flor. It was formed in the early fourteenth century, and its members played the dual role of pirates and privateers. At first, they were hired by the Byzantine Empire to combat Turkish advances. Soon after this, they turned to piracy and established a large presence in the Aegean and beyond.

The Catalan Company had military prowess. It led campaigns in Anatolia and managed a great victory at the Battle of Cyzicus in 1303. The company's members operated with a degree of independence and often engaged in looting and pillaging. They contributed to the devastation of local regions and established themselves as a powerful force in the Mediterranean. While the company was involved in local regional politics, it also significantly disrupted trade and local economies.

The aggressive maritime policies of the Crown of Aragon included outright piracy but also state-sponsored privateering. Yet again, the line between piracy and legitimate naval warfare significantly blurred. Piracy was a complex part of military and economic strategy at the time. The Crown's ability to leverage both official naval forces and private mercenary forces like the Catalan Company enabled it to exert considerable influence over Mediterranean politics.

Medieval Maritime Law: Efforts to Curb Piracy

This rise in piracy fueled the development of maritime laws and regulations that were aimed at curbing these types of activities. Several legal frameworks emerged across Europe that reflected the diverse and constantly evolving approaches to dealing with piracy.

The Laws of Oléron

Named after the Isle of Oléron, these laws established in the twelfth century were among the earliest known maritime codes. The laws weren't exclusively focused on piracy but provided guidelines for handling disputes and maintaining order on merchant vessels. They indirectly contributed to anti-piracy efforts by promoting safer and more regulated seafaring practices.

The Wisby Laws

The next important set of maritime regulations emerged from the town of Visby on the island of Gotland, Sweden. These were written in the thirteenth century and focused on commercial aspects of maritime activities. However, they also included measures to protect trade and navigation rights. This set of laws addressed some issues related to piracy by creating punishments for those who engaged in maritime theft and violence, helping to deter these types of activities.

Early Naval Efforts and Legal Measures

There were several approaches taken in medieval Europe to combat piracy. When looking at them, we can see the political and economic priorities of the different regions in how they approached piracy.

The Byzantine Empire

As mentioned, the Byzantines had a powerful navy but often negotiated with pirates. They found pirates useful and incorporated them into their empire's defense mechanisms in exchange for protection and legitimacy. It was a pragmatic approach. They managed to mitigate pirate threats while also leveraging their skills and expertise at sea.

Moorish Piracy

The Moorish pirates conducted raids for economic gain and as a form of warfare against Christian states. In response to this, Christian kingdoms used a mix of diplomacy, ransom payments, and military interventions to counter the threat.

Viking Raids

The response to Viking piracy varied widely. Some kingdoms responded by fortifying their coastlines and building defensive fleets. Others opted for more diplomatic solutions or paid tributes to buy peace.

Notable Medieval Pirates

Eustace the Monk

Eustace the monk was born Eustace Busket around 1170 in France. He led a life marked by some rather dramatic identity shifts. He initially joined the Benedictine monastery at St. Samer Abbey near Calais. His monastic life, however, was short-lived. Historical accounts suggest that he left the monastery around 1190. The reasoning for this was either to avenge his father's murder or due to a fallout related to family inheritance disputes.

The shift from a life dedicated to God to piracy was fueled by personal vendettas and political strife. Eustace failed to obtain justice for his father's murder. A later related dispute with Renaud de Dammartin, the Count of Boulogne, got him declared an outlaw. He hid in the Forest of Boulonnais and became a bandit, raiding the count's properties and engaging in a period of guerrilla-type warfare against the count that mirrors the legendary tales of Robin Hood.

By 1205, he had entered the service of King John of England. Eustace commanded a fleet of thirty ships and operated in the English Channel and the Strait of Dover. As a pirate, he preyed on French ships. However, he was a unique pirate. His strategic mind and ruthless tactics made him a valuable and feared asset to King John. He became known for attacking ships indiscriminately, including English vessels, and he did this without facing any reprimand from the English king.

Seven years later, he switched allegiances to King Philip II of France. It is said this was a strategic switch due to his personal vendetta against the Count of Boulogne. During the English Civil War, he supported the rebel barons and ferried Prince Louis of France across the channel. His naval expertise was a critical part in bringing reinforcements to the French cause. His incredible fortunes turned during the Battle of Sandwich in August 1217. His fleet was defeated by the English under Hubert de Burgh. Eustace was captured, having been found hiding in his ship's bilges. He was executed as he refused to bribe his way to freedom.

John Crabbe

From 1305 to 1352, John Crabbe was a famous Flemish pirate known for his ruthless raids in the North Sea and along the English Channel. His early exploits included capturing ships that were loaded with valuable cargo like wine and cloth. King Edward II of England regularly complained about John Crabbe, but he evaded justice for years. During the famine in 1316, he became an admiral of a fleet for Flanders, where he was charged with using piracy to secure food. He later switched his allegiance to Scotland and defended Berwick from English attacks. In an interesting twist of history, he eventually served King Edward III of England until his death in 1352.

Henry Paye

Also known as Harry Paye or Arriapye, this pirate from Poole, Dorset, was active in the late fourteenth and early fifteenth centuries. He started his career by raiding the coasts of France and Spain. He captured numerous ships and looted the coastal towns. One of his more notable moments was when he retaliated against a Franco-Spanish attack on Poole by capturing and bringing back 120 ships that were loaded with valuable goods. These daring exploits earned him a reputation as a pirate. He eventually became the Lord Warden of the Cinque Ports and continued to serve in that position until his death in 1419.

William Kyd

William served as a pirate from the mid-fifteenth century. He is remembered for his audacious acts of piracy along the English coast. In 1436, he captured the ship *Seynt Nunne* in Brittany, and in 1448, he took control of *La Marie* of London. But perhaps his most significant accomplishment came in 1453 when he captured *The Marie* of Saint Andrews. This prize came with a complicated legal dispute. The fate of William Kyd remains unclear.

Rollo (Göngu-Hrólfr)

Rollo, also known as Rollo the Walker, was a Viking who became the first Duke of Normandy. He was born around 846 CE and gained fame for his raids across the North Sea and into France. This included an attack on Paris. His exploits impressed King Charles the Simple of France so much that he granted Rollo land in Normandy in exchange for his loyalty and protection against other Viking raiders. This arrangement laid the foundation for the Duchy of Normandy. Rollo's descendants included William the Conqueror, would go on to play a significant role in European history.

Ragnar Lothbrok

Because this legendary Viking figure was known for his numerous raids across England and France during the ninth century, his life has been romanticized in sagas and popular culture—including a very popular TV show on the History Channel. He is attributed with the sack of Paris and the capture of various towns along the European coast. His legacy continued through his sons, who played prominent roles in Norse history. His son Bjorn also became a formidable raider; he conducted raids on the coast of Spain and North Africa. Bjorn's military campaigns extended the reach of Viking influence.

Chapter 3 – The Age of Exploration

The late Middle Ages experienced some significant changes when it came to maritime practices. All of these set the stage for the Age of Exploration. These shifts were characterized by advancements in naval technology, the rise of powerful nation-states, and the expanding horizons of European explorers. As feudalism began to decline and centralized monarchies grew, they began to invest in naval capabilities and overseas expeditions.

The late medieval period saw improvements in shipbuilding and navigation which were critical to the Age of Exploration. There were many innovations, like the caravel, a small highly maneuverable sailing ship. The development of the astrolabe and the magnetic compass allowed sailors to travel further and more safely than before. These technological advancements allowed the European explorers to take longer voyages that ultimately led to the discovery of new lands and new trade routes.

The fall of Constantinople in 1453 to the Ottoman Turks disrupted the more traditional trade routes between Europe and Asia. As a result, European powers had to seek alternative paths to the east. This shift incentivized exploration, which led to the subsequent colonization of new territories. Throw in the consolidation of power by monarchies in Spain, Portugal, and later England and France, and you have the financial and military support necessary to take on these more ambitious ventures.

As European nations vied for dominance in the new world, piracy became a tool for undermining their rivals and capturing valuable resources. State-sponsored privateers like the English sea dogs were authorized to attack enemy ships. Yet again, the Age of Exploration witnessed the rise of these notorious figures who exploited the chaotic and competitive nature of international trade.

Piracy in the New World

The discovery of the Americas changed piracy into a global enterprise. The New World was known for its vast wealth, particularly in silver and gold. This was an incredibly attractive prospect to pirates from across the globe. All the European powers were eager to exploit these resources for themselves. They built extensive trade networks that became prime targets for pirates both at home and abroad.

Spanish Treasure Fleets

The Spanish treasure fleet, also known as the West Indies Fleet (*Flota de Indias*) was a convoy system used by the Spanish Empire from 1566 to 1790. This fleet was designed to transport valuable goods between Spain and its American colonies. These ships were known to be full of gold, silver, precious stones, spices, and other valuable commodities.

The treasure fleet followed a well-organized system. Every year, two main fleets were dispatched. The New Spain fleet sailed to Veracruz, Mexico. The Tierra Firme fleet traveled to Cartagena and Portobelo in modern-day Colombia and Panama respectively. These fleets were set to gather goods from various colonies and then rendezvous in Havana, Cuba. Together, they formed a larger convoy for the return journey to Spain. These predictable operations were not the most intelligent move on Spain's part. A well-organized and repetitive system made them predictable, and these fleets very quickly became prime targets for pirates, state-sponsored privateers, and enemy naval forces. It did not matter that they had heavy fortifications and armed escorts. The following are some of the most notable attacks and confrontations.

Francis Drake's Capture of *Cacafuego* (1579)

While privateers were state-sponsored, they were in the end pirates. Francis Drake captured the Spanish galleon *Nuestra Señora de la Concepción*, also known as *Cacafuego*. This particular ship was heavily laden with silver and gold worth millions. This raid made Drake a hero in England and a feared pirate and criminal to the Spanish. This shows once again that the line between privateer and pirate is very fine.

Piet Hein's Capture of the New Spain Fleet (1628)

A Dutch pirate, Piet Pieterszoon Hein unexpectedly captured the entire New Spain treasure fleet near Cuba. This capture included an incredible amount of silver and other goods and delivered a severe blow to the Spanish economy. However, it gave a great boost to the Dutch war effort against Spain.

Thomas Cavendish and the *Santa Ana* (1587)

Thomas Cavendish was an English explorer and privateer/pirate who captured the Manila galleon *Santa Ana* off the coast of California. This particular ship carried cargo from the Philippines that included gold, silver, and silks, which goes to show the amount of wealth that was being transported by these fleets.

Spanish Attempts at Defense

Spain attempted to protect these ships full of valuable cargo. But these pirates and privateers were formidable opponents, and not many of these strategies worked. The first attempt was the convoy system, in which treasure trips always traveled in large convoys that were accompanied by heavily armed warships. But as we can see from the previous examples, this did not always deter the pirates. In fact, many of the pirates also possessed heavily armed ships.

In 1521, Spain established the Armada de la Guarda de la Carrera de Indias. This was a fleet of warships that patrolled the waters between the Azores and Spain. They later expanded the protection area to cover the entire route from the Caribbean to Europe.

But it wasn't only the ships that the pirates targeted. Because ports like Veracruz, Portobelo, and Cartagena served as collection points for the fleets, the pirates would attack them as well. Spain began to heavily fortify these key ports to thwart the pirates.

Spain relied heavily on the wealth that was extracted from its colonies abroad. These treasure ships were so important that the loss of even one would have a devastating impact on Spain's economy. This reliance made the protection of these ships a top priority. Spain had to invest a significant amount of money in their naval defenses and fortifications because of piracy.

Piracy in the Old World during the Age of Exploration

In addition to the new acts of piracy in the New World, piracy continued to be an issue in the Old World. The increased maritime trade between Europe, Africa, and Asia provided numerous opportunities for pirates to attack merchant vessels and disrupt trade routes on a more local scale.

In the Mediterranean, piracy continued to be rampant, particularly along the North African coast. The barbary corsairs who operated out of ports like Algiers, Tunis, and Tripoli were notorious for their attacks on European shipping. Much like other pirates, these corsairs were often sanctioned by local rulers. They captured ships and enslaved their crews. Those who were worth something were ransomed back for their release; the others were sold as slaves on the market. The scale of piracy in the Mediterranean inspired many of the European powers to launch punitive expeditions. However, these efforts were often only temporary solutions to a much larger problem.

The Indian Ocean and Red Sea also became hot spots for piracy. Pirates from the Arabian Peninsula and the Horn of Africa targeted these lucrative trade routes that developed between the Middle East, India, and East Africa. These pirates attacked both Muslim and European ships. It was easy for them to take advantage of the rich commerce and spices, textiles, and other valuable goods. Colonial powers, such as the Portuguese, established naval patrols to protect their interests. Despite many of these efforts, piracy remained a persistent threat.

In Northern Europe, the English Channel and the North Sea became frequent targets for pirates and privateers. The English, French, and Dutch governments all issued letters of marque that allowed privateers to legally attack enemy ships during wartime, maintaining the common practice of blurring the lines between piracy and state-sanctioned privateering.

Lastly, the Baltic Sea also experienced a rise in piracy, particularly from the Hanseatic League cities. These were major training hubs during the medieval and early modern periods. Many pirates, including the infamous Victual Brothers, disrupted the trade routes by attacking merchant vessels. As the Hanseatic League declined and powerful nation-states came into being, the region developed greater naval patrols and more efforts to combat piracy.

European Colonial Powers and Their Contribution to the Rise of Piracy

Spain

Spain dominated the Americas rather early on. They inadvertently fostered piracy because of the vast and wealthy colonies they developed. As mentioned earlier, Spanish treasure fleets became prime targets for pirates and privateers. These attacks were not just acts of piracy but part of a broader geopolitical strategy. Rival nations frequently sought to weaken Spain's economic power by targeting its treasure convoys.

England

England's approach to piracy was a little more strategic. England very frequently hired pirates, essentially turning them into state-sponsored privateers, making them sound slightly less criminal. These privateers' sole purpose was to harass Spanish shipping efforts. Figures like Sir Francis Drake were knighted for their exploits against Spanish interests. These state-sanctioned pirates also played a key role in England's strategy during conflicts like the Anglo-Spanish War. The government gave letters of marque or legal documents that authorized these pirates to attack enemy ships.

English privateers targeted the Spanish treasure fleets, but they also established bases in the Caribbean. These bases allowed them to launch further raids and helped England weaken Spanish dominance. The use of legalized piracy eventually allowed England to establish its own colonies in the New World.

France

France also used piracy and privateering to undermine its rivals. When it came to international trade, its rival was predominantly Spain. French privateers were also known as corsairs and operated out of ports like Saint-Malo and Dunkirk. They initially attacked only Spanish vessels but later took on the English shipping industry as it grew. As with the other nations, the French Crown supported these activities and viewed them as a rather cost-effective way to disrupt its enemies' trade. Not only was this strategy taking down its enemies; it was also enriching the state without the expense of maintaining a large navy.

The French colonization efforts in the Caribbean and North America were often accompanied by piracy. Islands like Tortuga became infamous pirate havens. French buccaneers launched raids from these islands against Spanish ships and settlements. It's a perfect example of the complex relationship between piracy and colonial expansion. The French pirates played a dual role of plundering and protecting French colonial interests.

Noteworthy Pirates of the Age of Exploration

Sir Francis Drake

Sir Francis Drake (c. 1540-1596) was an English sea captain, privateer, and navigator. He was born in Devonshire, England, and began his seafaring career in his late teens. Drake became rather prominent because of his daring exploits against the Spanish empire. Queen Elizabeth I commissioned Drake as a privateer, and he was authorized to plunder Spanish ships and settlements. Effectively, Drake was a state-sanctioned pirate.

His most famous exploit in 1572 would be his raid on the Spanish port of Nombre de Dios. He also circumnavigated the globe between 1577 and 1580. While completing this incredible adventure, he captured numerous Spanish vessels and amassed significant wealth and prestige. He was celebrated in England and knighted by Queen Elizabeth I aboard his ship, the *Golden Hind,* upon his return. His actions significantly weakened Spanish dominance in the New World and contributed to the continuing conflict between England and Spain. This ultimately ended with the defeat of the Spanish Armada in 1588.

Sir Martin Frobisher

Sir Martin Frobisher (c. 1535-1594) was another noteworthy English pirate and explorer during the Age of Exploration. Initially, he set out to find the Northwest Passage to Asia. His voyages primarily led to the Arctic regions. He made multiple expeditions in search of gold, which yielded very little in terms of precious metals. However, he was recognized for his contributions to English maritime exploration.

In the end, he was a pirate. He engaged in privateering, targeting Spanish ships and contributing to England's naval efforts against Spain. He served as vice admiral under Sir Francis Drake, and his naval experience and leadership were an important part of the English victory over the Spanish Armada. His legacy is a blend of exploration and piracy, which serves to highlight the dual roles many of the maritime figures played during this period.

Sir Walter Raleigh

Sir Walter Raleigh (c. 1552–1618) is probably more well-known for his writing, but he was also an English explorer and soldier and played a key role in the Elizabethan colonization of North America. He is best known for his efforts to establish English colonies in the New World. Raleigh is the one who sponsored the ill-fated Roanoke Colony that mysteriously disappeared. Raleigh also engaged in privateering against Spanish interests and captured numerous vessels, amassing considerable wealth.

His ambitions and actions often got him into trouble with powerful figures at court. Eventually, he was imprisoned in the Tower of London. His fortunes fluctuated regularly, but his contributions to English exploration and his involvement in the early colonial efforts left a lasting impact on the history of the New World.

Grace O'Malley

Not all the colonies established at this time were across the Atlantic Ocean. Grace O'Malley (c. 1530–1603), also known as Gráinne Mhaol, was an Irish pirate and chieftain who defied the English authorities in Ireland. Grace was born into the powerful O'Malley clan in County Mayo. A woman out of her time, she commanded a fleet of ships and engaged in piracy and trade along the Irish coast. She was an incredible ship captain, and her leadership earned her a reputation as a formidable figure who was both feared and respected by her contemporaries.

Her open defiance of English rule and her negotiation with Queen Elizabeth I in 1593 showcased her political intelligence and her ability to navigate the complex power dynamics of the time. Despite being a pirate, Grace O'Malley is remembered as a symbol of resistance against English domination and a significant figure in Irish history.

William Dampier

William Dampier (1651–1715) was another English explorer, pirate, and naturalist. His detailed journals provide valuable insights into the Age of Exploration. He initially engaged in piracy by raiding Spanish ships and settlements in the Caribbean and the Pacific. However, this shifted as his keen observations and writings about the natural world distinguished him from other pirates of his time.

His extensive travels took him all around the globe, and his works influenced other figures like Jonathan Swift and Daniel Defoe. He made incredible contributions to navigation, hydrography, and natural history, becoming one of the most respected figures among the early explorers and pirates.

The Victual Brothers

The Victual Brothers, or *Vitalienbrüder*, started as a group of privateers in the late fourteenth century. They were initially hired in 1392 by the Dukes of Mecklenburg to support their fight against Queen Margaret I of Denmark. The name "Victual Brothers" comes from their original mission to supply (victual) the besieged city of Stockholm.

Like many mercenaries, after the conflict ended, they had to change professions to maintain their way of life. They began to target merchant ships and raid coastal towns in the Baltic Sea and the North Sea and quickly became a significant threat to maritime trade in the region. They were very capable of launching well-coordinated and devastating assaults on key economic centers, including the sacking of the important trading town of Bergen in 1393.

One of their most famous leaders was Klaus Störtebeker. His exploits became legendary, and he earned a reputation not far off from that of a folk hero. His name translates to "drink the beaker empty" and allegedly referred to his ability to consume large quantities of beer without stopping. Under his command, the Victual Brothers maintained their acts of piracy and captured numerous vessels, amassing substantial wealth. Störtebeker's life ended abruptly when he was captured and executed in Hamburg in 1401. The legend around his death states that after being beheaded, his body supposedly walked past several of his crew members. This act is said to have spared their execution, but in fact, they were executed anyway.

Following his death, the members of the Victual Brothers that remained organized themselves into a group known as the *Likedeelers*, or "equal sharers." This new name reflected their practice of equally distributing the spoils of their raids among themselves. They continued their piratical activities well into the fifteenth century in the Baltic and North Seas.

The Victual Brothers are remembered not only for their piracy but also for their defiance against the established authorities, democratic organization, and fierce independence. They often clashed with the

Hanseatic League. This was a tumultuous era, and they caused some serious trouble when it came to maritime trade.

Chapter 4 – The Golden Age of Piracy

From 1650 to 1730 was what historians call the Golden Age of Piracy. This was a time when maritime piracy was at its peak and impacted the trade routes and colonial enterprises across the globe. This era also saw the rise of some of the most infamous pirates who operated in regions like the Caribbean, the American coast, and the Indian Ocean.

Timeline

The Golden Age of Piracy is often divided into three periods:

1. **Buccaneering Period (1650-1680):** This period marked the rise of Buccaneers. These seamen, primarily of French and English origin, were based in the Caribbean—more particularly on the islands of Tortuga and Jamaica. Buccaneers initially targeted Spanish shipping and settlements in the Caribbean, where they exploited the incredible wealth of the Spanish Empire.

2. **Pirate Round (1690s):** During this decade, English pirates began to sail the Indian Ocean and the Red Sea. They attacked Mughal and other merchant vessels. Notable pirates like Henry Every and William Kidd operated during this time. They targeted richly laden ships that were traveling between the Indian subcontinent and the Middle East.

3. **Post-Spanish Succession Period (1716-1726):** After the end of the War of Spanish Succession, things heated up again. Many

sailors and privateers were displaced by the end of the war and turned to piracy. This led to the resurgence of pirate activities in in the Caribbean and along the American eastern seaboard.

Major Areas of Activity

1. **The Caribbean:** The Caribbean remained a hotbed and epicenter of pirate activity throughout the Golden Age. Pirates like Blackbeard (Edward Teach), Bartholomew Roberts, and Charles Vane sailed these waters and preyed on merchant ships. They established personal bases on islands such as New Providence (Nassau) in the Bahamas and Tortuga. The Caribbean's natural geography, with numerous small islands and hidden coves, provided pirates with strategic positions along major shipping routes. The Caribbean was the ideal pirate haven.

2. **The American Coast:** The eastern coast of North America, from the Carolinas to New England, was also a prime spot for pirate activities. Ports like Charleston and Boston were frequented by pirates. They went to these ports to sell their plunder and recruit new members. While pirates sold their goods in American ports, the dense shipping traffic along the coast also provided them with several opportunities to capture more valuable cargo.

3. **The Indian Ocean:** The Indian Ocean had several rich trade routes between Europe, Africa, and Asia. Pirates captured treasure-laden ships traveling from the Mughal Empire and the East Indies. Madagascar became a pirate haven and served as the base for many of these Indian Ocean pirates, providing a strategic location for launching raids and hiding from naval patrols.

The Rise of the Pirate

The constant conflicts between the European powers, including the Anglo-Spanish War and the War of Spanish Succession, created a surplus of experienced sailors who had nothing to do during peacetime. This also followed an intense time when letters of marque issued during wartime blurred the lines between privateering and piracy.

Many privateers continued their activities. Not doing so would mean significantly minimizing their wealth and achievements. Piracy promised a life of wealth with a side of rebellion. Many also felt stifled and held back by the rigid social hierarchies of the time, and turning to piracy was an instantaneous act against society.

The expansion of global trade routes created more and more targets for pirates. Beyond Spanish treasure fleets, ships carrying valuable cargoes with gold, silver, spices, and textiles were irresistible to the pirates and mercenaries-turned-pirates looking to make a quick fortune.

Once they were no longer at war, these European powers weren't investing as much into their naval patrols. This meant that pirates could operate relatively freely. It is believed that there were over 5000 pirates roaming the sea at any time during this period.

These powers had stretched themselves so thin that their colonies were also not well maintained. Pirates easily established bases in areas that had limited or ineffective colonial governance. These little havens provided safe anchorages, supplies, and markets for selling their plundered goods. There was very little law, control, or surveillance. The most famous pirate havens would include Port Royal in Jamaica, Nassau in the Bahamas, and St. Mary's Island off Madagascar.

Famous Pirate Havens

Nassau: The Pirate Republic

Nassau sat on New Providence Island in the Bahamas. It was initially a British settlement that was abandoned on several occasions due to attacks by the Spanish and French forces. By 1713, it had been taken by pirates and transformed into a bustling hub of piratical activity. It became famously known as the "Republic of Pirates." The city was located at a strategic location along key shipping routes. It had a natural harbor with shallow waters, making it an ideal base for pirate operations. Larger naval vessels found great difficulty trying to navigate these waters, which provided the pirates with a natural defense against anyone who might pursue them.

Benjamin Hornigold and a few others were instrumental in establishing Nassau as a pirate haven. Under his influence, Nassau attracted quite a few notorious pirates, including Blackbeard, Charles Vane, and Calico Jack. These pirates operated under a loose confederation. They followed a "pirate code" or "articles of agreement" that governed their behavior and operations.

During the height of its pirate activity, Nassau became a city of lawlessness with a unique sense of community. The population of pirates in Nassau often outnumbered the local residents. This created a dynamic but volatile atmosphere. The pirates frequented the taverns and brothels and spent their loot on revelry. They established a unique culture of storytelling and bravado.

The locals didn't seem to mind much because the pirate economy supported the local businesses and an incredibly diverse population that included individuals from Europe, Africa, and the Americas.

This didn't mean life was easy. Life was harsh, and any disputes on the island were often settled with violence.

The Republic of Pirates in Nassau began to decline in 1718 when the British Crown appointed Woodes Rogers as the royal governor of the Bahamas. The major trading nations pressured the English Crown to do something about the pirate problem. Rogers arrived in the Bahamas with a fleet of Royal Navy ships. His job was simple: restore law and order. He didn't come in with guns blazing, though. He offered a royal pardon to pirates who surrendered. This led to a mixed response from the pirate community. Prominent pirates like Benjamin Hornigold accepted the pardon and even helped Rogers hunt down those who refused to comply.

Rogers was relentless. He successfully dismantled the pirate stronghold and captured and executed several pirates. Famous pirates like Blackbeard and Charles Vane met their demise either in battle or through execution. This was the end of Nassau's era as a pirate republic.

Tortuga: The Buccaneer's Sanctuary

Tortuga is an island off the northern coast of Hispaniola (modern-day Haiti) that was a significant pirate haven during the seventeenth century. The island was initially settled by French hunters known as Buccaneers. It evolved into a pirate stronghold around 1630 because of its strategic location and defensible harbor. It was an ideal place to launch attacks on the Spanish shipping lines.

Jean Le Vasseur, a French engineer and adventurer, led the island's transformation into a pirate haven. He seized control of the island in the early 1640s and built Fort de Rocher, overlooking the main harbor. The fort was designed to protect the harbor against Spanish incursions and simultaneously established Tortuga as a secure base for pirates. By constructing the fort, Vasseur solidified the island's status as a hub for piracy. It began to attract more buccaneers and privateers from various nations, including France, England, and the Netherlands.

The pirates of Tortuga formed a loose coalition that they called the "Brethren of the Coast." This fraternity was made up of mostly French and English buccaneers who operated under a common code of conduct that emphasized shared decision-making, hierarchical command structures, and equitable division of plunder. The Brethren often received privateer commissions from European powers to target Spanish treasure ships. They operated with a thin veneer of legitimacy, yet again blurring the lines between piracy and privateering.

The Brethren were not just pirates. They also engaged in trading goods like ginger and tobacco with Dutch merchants, who in turn provided them with supplies and slaves. This black-market trade contributed to the economic success of Tortuga. It became a thriving and bustling pirate enclave.

Unlike other pirate havens, the influence of Tortuga's pirates started to wane toward the end of the seventeenth century. Increased military efforts by the Spanish and the establishment of other pirate havens at Port Royal in Jamaica contributed to this decline. The end of major European conflicts also reduced the need for privateering, which provided a cover for many of their activities.

By the early eighteenth century, Tortuga's peak as a pirate haven was over, yet it remained a symbol of the golden age of buccaneering. The legacy of Tortuga lives on in popular culture and pirate lore. Tortuga has become a symbol of the lawlessness and adventurous spirit of the era.

Madagascar: Pirate Haven in the Indian Ocean

The European powers had tried to colonize Madagascar on numerous occasions, but all their efforts were largely unsuccessful. The English tried to establish a colony at Saint Augustine Bay in 1644. They were thwarted easily by the harsh conditions and hostile encounters with local tribes. The French managed to maintain a small settlement at Fort Dauphin from 1643 until the locals destroyed it in 1674.

Even with these failures, the island's strategic location and resources made it attractive to pirates who were looking for a base of operations. The island has several harbors, an abundance of freshwater, and no central authority at the time, making it an ideal refuge for these outlaws. The island's ports were secluded coves and offered ways to get fresh supplies. It was an ideal location for careening ships, recruiting crew members, and then treating their plundered goods.

From around 1690 to 1723, Madagascar was a key hub for pirates, in particular, those involved in the "Pirate Round." This was a route that began in the western Atlantic, rounded the Cape of Good Hope, and ventured into the Indian Ocean. This route had been pioneered by pirates like Thomas Tew, who gained great wealth by attacking ships traveling between India and the Middle East.

One of the most intriguing stories associated with Madagascar is that of Libertalia. This was a supposed anarchist colony founded by pirates under the leadership of Captain James Mission. According to the book *A General History of the Pyrates* by Captain Charles Johnson, Libertalia operated on the principles of egalitarianism and shared wealth. These concepts attracted pirates who were disillusioned with the hierarchical structures of the time. The existence of Libertalia is debated, but the myth reflects the desire for a more utopian society free from the constraints of European colonial powers.

By 1711, the number of pirates in Madagascar had dwindled significantly. Many of the pirates accepted offers of pardon from the European governments to avoid execution. They also fought with increased naval patrols by the British East India Company and other forces in the Indian Ocean, which made piracy more dangerous and less profitable. Native Indian pirates also began to dominate the region, which reduced the opportunities for European pirates. This marked the end of Madagascar's prominence as a pirate haven.

Chapter 5 – Infamous Pirates of the Golden Age

Blackbeard (Edward Teach)

Edward Teach, better known to many as Blackbeard the infamous pirate, was born around 1680. Little is known about his early life beyond that he was probably born in Bristol, England. It is believed he began his seafaring career as a privateer during the War of the Spanish Succession (1701-1713). Like many privateers, after the war, he turned to piracy. He started by joining the crew of the notorious pirate captain Benjamin Hornigold around 1716. Hornigold very quickly put Teach in command of his own ship, marking the beginning of his notorious pirate career.

It was in November 1717 that Blackbeard captured the large French slave ship, *La Concorde*. He refitted this ship and named it *Queen Anne's Revenge*. This ship became his flagship and one of the most feared pirate vessels of the time. It boasted forty guns and a crew of over 300 men. His fearsome reputation was only enhanced by his choice of appearance. He sported a long black beard that he tied with ribbons lit with slow-burning fuses during battles to create a terrifying image.

An illustration of Blackbeard.[1]

Perhaps his most famous exploit was the blockade of Charleston, South Carolina, in May 1718, in which he captured nine vessels attempting to enter or leave the port. He held prominent citizens hostage and demanded a chest of medicine as ransom—an interesting ransom for a pirate, but medicine was as good as gold at this time. It was a bold move that demonstrated his power and audacity. Blackbeard was known for striking fear into the hearts of his enemies, and this move only solidified his legendary status.

In June 1718, Blackbeard deliberately ran *Queen Anne's Revenge* aground near Beaufort Inlet, North Carolina. The reasons for this action are unknown, but it was possible he was trying to reduce the number of his crew and escape with the bulk of the loot. He accepted a royal pardon from Governor Charles Eden of North Carolina, but this didn't last long. He quickly returned to piracy and used his remaining sloop, the *Adventure*, to continue his raids.

Blackbeard continued to be incredibly bold, and this drew the attention of Alexander Spotswood, the governor of Virginia, who sent a naval expedition to capture Blackbeard. On November 22, 1718, Blackbeard was cornered off Ocracoke Island by a force led by Lieutenant Robert Maynard. Blackbeard was killed in a fierce battle after sustaining multiple gunshot and sword wounds. His head was severed from his body and hung from Maynard's bowsprit as a grim trophy and warning to all other pirates.

Blackbeard's career as a pirate was relatively short, but his impact on pirate lore is intense. His fearsome image, daring exploits, and the dramatic end he came to have cemented his place as one of the most infamous pirates in history. His story has been romanticized and mythologized in several books, movies, and other media. He is an enduring symbol of the Golden Age of Piracy.

Calico Jack (John Rackham)

John Rackham, who was more popularly known as Calico Jack, was born on December 26, 1682, in England. He earned the nickname Calico Jack because he preferred to wear brightly colored calico clothing. We don't know much about his early life. He didn't hit the history books until 1718 while serving as the quartermaster under the infamous pirate captain Charles Vane. Calico Jack rose in the ranks after he led a mutiny against Vane. He was able to win the crew to his side after Vane refused to engage a French warship. After the successful mutiny, Rackham was elected their new captain and Vane was marooned with his few loyal followers.

Calico Jack was a bold pirate captain. His ambitions weren't always successful but did pay off frequently enough to please the crew. Rackham and his crew were able to capture the merchant ship *Kingston* off the coast of Port Royal, Jamaica. The merchants that owned this ship hired bounty hunters to chase after them. Three months later, they found them at Isla de Pinos (now Isla de la Juventud), just south of Cuba. While Calico Jack and most of his crew were ashore, the bounty hunters captured their ship and forced the pirates to flee into the woods.

Rackham and his men made their way back to Nassau. There, they convinced Governor Woodes Rogers to grant them a pardon by claiming that Vane had forced them all into piracy. Like many pirates, his time as an honest man was short. Very quickly, life back in society lost its appeal, and he returned to piracy, joined by Anne Bonny and Mary Read, another female pirate. Allegedly, John Rackham and Anne Bonny began a romantic relationship. In 1720, the three of them, with a small crew, stole a ship and slipped out of Nassau under the cover of darkness. They terrorized the waters off Jamaica for three months, attacking fishing boats and lightly armed merchant vessels. By October 1720, the pirate hunter Jonathan Barnet, under the orders of the governor of Jamaica (Sir Nicholas Lawes), tracked them down and captured them. Rackham and his crew were hiding below deck and were said to be drunk. As the story goes, Bonnie and Read, along with one other pirate, were the only ones continuing to resist.

Rackham and his crew were taken to Spanish Town, Jamaica, where they were swiftly tried and convicted of piracy. Rackham pled innocence but was found guilty because of an overwhelming abundance of evidence against him. On November 18, 1720, Rackham was hanged at Gallows Point in Port Royal. His body was gibbeted (the display of a hanged body by hanging them by chains) at a small islet that's now known as Rackham's Cay as a warning to all other pirates. Both Mary Read and Anne Bonny escaped execution by claiming to be pregnant. (Pregnancy at this time provided women with a temporary stay of execution.) Mary Reed died in prison, but Anne Bonny's fate remains a mystery.

Anne Bonny

Anne Bonny was born around 1700 in Ireland. She was the illegitimate daughter of lawyer William Cormack and his servant, Mary Brennan. To escape the scandal, he moved his family to Charles Town (now Charleston), South Carolina. He gave up his life as a solicitor and became a successful merchant. Anne's mother died when she was twelve.

Anne's fiery temper became evident very early on, and there are tales of her setting fire to her father's plantation in retaliation for an unknown slight. Much of what we know about Anne Bonny comes from sources that aren't reliable, so we have to rely on tales to piece together a possible life story. In her late teens, she married a small-time pirate named James Bonny. Her father did not approve of the marriage and subsequently disowned her. Anne and her new husband moved to Nassau in the Bahamas. She often mingled with the other pirates in Nassau's Taverns and eventually met the pirate John "Calico Jack" Rackham.

As mentioned previously, she joined his crew. Anne was known for donning men's clothes during battle and was notorious for her fierce demeanor and combat skills. During one of their acts of thievery, Rackham's crew captured a ship that was carrying Mary Read, who was also dressed as a man. Anne and Mary became very close and formed a formidable partnership within Rackham's crew. The presence of these two women was very unusual in the male-dominated world of piracy. However, both women earned respect through their bravery and combat skills.

As mentioned earlier, Anne Bonny was found guilty of piracy but received a stay of execution after claiming she was pregnant. Her fate is unclear. It's possible she was released, escaped, or died in prison. Some accounts suggest that she returned to South Carolina and lived out her days under a different name. All these possibilities are speculative.

Mary Read

Mary Reed was born around 1692 in England. Like Anne Bonny, much of her life is hard to piece together due to the many stories that grew around her.

She had a very unconventional upbringing. Much like Anne, she was the illegitimate daughter of Polly Read. Polly disguised Mary as her deceased half-brother to secure financial support from her late husband's family. Mary continued to dress as a man well into adulthood. She initially worked as a footman and later joined the British military. During her military service in Flanders, she fell in love with another soldier. She revealed her identity, and they married. Together, they ran an inn until he died.

After her husband died, Mary returned to dressing as a man and enlisted in the Dutch military. She eventually got aboard a ship that was bound for the West Indies. Unfortunately, this ship was captured by pirates. Mary was intrigued by their way of life. She decided to join the pirates and very quickly became a formidable figure herself.

Like many others, in 1718, she accepted a royal pardon, but this did not last long. Shortly after, she joined Calico Jack's crew and met Anne Bonny, who would become her dear friend. Some claim that Mary and Anne became lovers. Their secret identities as women were revealed to the crew over time. By that point, their prowess in battle had earned them respect and fear among the crew.

As mentioned previously, Mary claimed to be pregnant when they were finally caught but died from a fever in prison in April 1721. Her life has been romanticized in various books, films, and other media. She boldly defined the gender norms of the period and had an adventurous spirit that cemented her place in pirate lore. She is one of the most legendary female pirates of the Golden Age of Piracy.

Charles Vane

Charles Vane is known as one of the most vicious English pirates active during the Golden Age of Piracy. His exploits occurred between 1716 and 1720. Like many pirates, little is known about his early life. His name appeared in the history books during the War of Spanish Succession, and he later joined the crew of Henry Jennings and the Flying Gang. One of his first large acts as a pirate was raiding the salvage camp of the 1715 Spanish treasure fleet off the coast of Florida. This won him a substantial amount of gold and silver

Vane was known to be ruthless. His tactics were cruel, and he often tortured the captured sailors during his exploits and failed to follow the pirate code. This frequently created tension among his crew. Unlike many others, he refused to accept the king's pardon for pirates in 1718. After refusing the pardon, Vane led a small fleet and became a dominant figure in Nassau, challenging British authority. He once set a ship aflame and used it as a fireship against the British blockade. His crew mutinied against him later that year because he decided to retreat from an engagement with a powerful French frigate.

Losing his ship and crew didn't stop Vane. He continued his piratical activities with the small band of followers that were marooned alongside him. A hurricane in 1719 shipwrecked Vane on an uninhabited island in the Bay of Honduras. He tried to join a passing British ship's crew under a false name, but he was eventually recognized by an old acquaintance and captured. He was taken to Jamaica, where he was tried and found guilty of piracy. The infamous Charles Vane was hanged in March 1721. His body was displayed in chains as a warning to other would-be pirates.

Henry Morgan

Henry Morgan was a Welshman born around 1635. He rose in the history books as one of the most famous privateers and buccaneers of the seventeenth century. It's believed he arrived in the Caribbean as part of an English military expedition that was led by General Venables and

Admiral Penn. They captured Jamaica from the Spanish in 1655.

Morgan began his career as a privateer under Sir Christopher Myngs. He participated in several raids against Spanish settlements in the Caribbean and Central America. His most notable exploits include the attacks on Portobelo, Maracaibo, and Panama. When he took Portobello in 1668, he captured the town and demanded a ransom of 100,000 pesos to spare it from being destroyed. This particular attack bolstered his reputation as well as his wealth. He became a legend among buccaneers.

When Morgan took on Maracaibo in 1669, he cleverly outmaneuvered a Spanish fleet by using a disguised fireship. He successfully captured one Spanish warship and destroyed another. He and his men were able to plunder Maracaibo and Gibraltar, which earned them a substantial haul of silver and other valuables.

Perhaps his most ambitious raid came in 1671 when he attacked Panama City. At this time, it was the wealthiest city in the new world. He successfully captured the heavily fortified San Lorenzo fortress, and then his forces marched through the jungle and overwhelmed the city's defenders. They gained access to the city and took it over, but most of the treasure had already been evacuated. It was far less profitable than they expected.

Henry Morgan transitioned from privateering to a more legitimate role later in life. He was knighted by King Charles II and appointed lieutenant governor of Jamaica. He played a role in the island's defense and governance until his death in 1688.

Stede Bonnet

Stede Bonnet, a gentleman in many ways, was not a very good pirate. He led a unique and tragic career in piracy during the early eighteenth century.

Bonnet was born around 1688 to a wealthy family on the island of Barbados. He inherited a substantial estate after his parents' early death, and his life was relatively comfortable. He served as a major in the British Army before settling into being a plantation owner.

But something happened in 1717. Bonnet inexplicably decided to abandon his comfortable life as a plantation owner and pursue piracy. He made this choice without any maritime experience. He purchased a sloop, the *Revenge*, and outfitted it with ten guns and a crew of about seventy men. He told the local authorities that he was going to act as a privateer but very quickly turned to piracy. He captured several ships along the eastern seaboard of the American colonies.

A combination of his lack of seafaring skills and eccentric behavior made him a very unusual and often ineffective pirate leader. It's even said that he would walk around deck in his nightgown.

In a twist of fate, Bonnet met the infamous pirate Blackbeard in 1717. Blackbeard very quickly recognized Bonnet's incompetence and took command of the *Revenge.* This new partnership was marked by Blackbeard's dominance and Bonnet's subjugation. Eventually, Blackbeard betrayed Bonnet and marooned some of his crew while absconding with all the loot.

Bonnet was left trying to redeem his pirate career. He later resumed command of the *Revenge* under the alias "Captain Thomas." He renamed it the *Royal James* and continued his piratical activities. Although he captured several more vessels, his renewed efforts were short-lived. In September 1718, Colonel William Rhett was tasked with hunting down pirates and capturing Bonnet at the Cape Fear River. Bonnet didn't go down without a decent fight that ended in both sides running aground. Bonnet was taken to Charleston, South Carolina,

An engraving of Stede Bonnet.[2]

where he was tried and found guilty of piracy and murder. He begged for mercy but was eventually hanged on December 10, 1718.

While most pirates had an obvious reason for turning to piracy, Bonnet's motivations were unclear. His life as a pirate was marked by misadventure and ended in failure and execution. His story is one of the more curious episodes in the annals of piracy.

Thomas Tew

Thomas Tew is often referred to as the "Rhode Island Pirate." He was born sometime in the late seventeenth century, and his career in piracy is well recorded, unlike his early life. He began his maritime career as a privateer. In 1692, he received a letter of marque from the governor of Bermuda. It was his job to raid French shipping. However, he and his crew soon decided to abandon this commission and turn to outright piracy. They set sail on the *Amity* and captured a large Indian ship in the Red Sea that was laden with gold, silver, ivory, and many other treasures. This haul alone made him very wealthy and famous. His share was estimated to be about 8,000 pounds, which was a significant fortune at the time.

This initial success encouraged Thomas to take on a second voyage in 1694. He received another privateering commission from Governor Benjamin Fletcher of New York. The intent was to raid the Mughal Empire's treasure ships. This time he joined forces with other pirates, including Henry Every. In September 1695, during an attempt to capture the Mughal convoy, he was killed by cannon fire. His death inspired the rest of his crew to surrender.

Despite his gruesome death, Thomas Tew was one of the pioneers of the Pirate Round and significantly impacted the establishment of pirate havens like Madagascar.

William Kidd (Captain Kidd)

Captain Kidd, or William Kidd, was a Scottish privateer who became infamous for turning to piracy. He was born in Dundee, Scotland, around 1654. Initially, he built a reputation as a successful privateer. In 1696, he was given the task of hunting down pirates in the Indian Ocean and was funded by a group of powerful English investors that included Lord Belmont, who was then the governor of New York, Massachusetts, and New Hampshire.

Kidd set sail on *Adventure Galley*, a heavily armed ship, with the high hopes of capturing pirates and French vessels. This voyage was plagued by misfortune. He struggled repeatedly to find legitimate targets, and this led to considerable discontent among his crew. His crew eventually mutinied in 1697, and Kidd was forced to kill his gunner, William Moore.

By 1698, it seemed that Kidd's luck was changing. He captured the *Quedagh Merchant*, a ship full of valuable cargo. However, this act, along with his previous attack on a Portuguese vessel and his association with pirate Robert Culliford, sealed his fate as a pirate in the eyes of British authorities. All his sponsors chose to distance themselves from Kidd and push for his arrest.

The next year, he sailed to Boston to clear his name. Unfortunately, he was arrested and sent back to England, where he faced a highly publicized trial. He claimed that he acted under duress and within the bounds of his commission, but he was still found guilty of piracy and the murder of Moore. He was hanged in 1701.

The legend of Captain Kidd endures. In particular, there are many stories of his buried treasure, which have inspired countless treasure hunts and works of fiction. In truth, Captain Kidd may have been one of the unluckiest pirates in history. He suffered from the misfortune of becoming a privateer/pirate right at the time when the privateer/pirate was considered an outlaw.

Henry Every

Henry Every was known by many names, including Henry Avery, Long Ben, or John Avery. He's among the most infamous and successful pirates during the Golden Age of Piracy. Born in Devon, England, around 1659, he first served in the Royal Navy and later in the Atlantic slave trade. He transitioned into piracy around 1694 when he led a mutiny aboard the privateering ship *Charles II*, which he then renamed *Fancy*.

Henry completed his most notable act of piracy in 1695 when he captured the *Ganj-i-Sawai*, a Mughal treasure ship, off the coast of Yemen. The ship was en route from the seaport of Mocha, Yemen, to Surat, India, and was laden with gold, silver, and precious gems. This raid was brutal and involved torturing and killing many of the passengers. It resulted in a treasure haul worth an estimated 325,000 pounds at the time. This would be equivalent to millions today.

The capture of this ship started a diplomatic crisis between the Mughal Empire and the British government. There were some severe repercussions for the English East India Company. The Mughal emperor Aurangzeb demanded that Henry Every and his crew be captured, so the British government immediately issued a large bounty on Every's head. There was a massive manhunt, but Every evaded it and disappeared from history. Some say he fled to Ireland, but ultimately his fate remains a mystery of history.

Henry Every's story has become the stuff of legend and inspired many works of fiction. He very easily cemented his legacy as one of the most successful pirates of all time with one notable event.

Edward England

Edward England was born Edward Seegar around 1685 in Ireland. He began his pirating career in the Caribbean, eastern Atlantic, and Indian Ocean between 1717 and 1720. He first served as the first mate on a sloop that was captured by pirates led by Captain Christopher Winter. He was quickly embraced by his captor and rose through the ranks, eventually captaining his own ship.

One of England's most famous ships was the *Fancy* (named in honor of the legendary Henry Every), a thirty-four-cannon Dutch frigate he had captured. Unlike other pirates, England was known for his humane treatment of prisoners. However, this was a quality that often put him at odds with his crew.

England was a successful pirate. He and his crew captured several ships, including a Portuguese ship near the Mascarene Islands, which was carrying a large amount of valuable goods and the viceroy of Portuguese Goa. His most famous capture was with the British East India Company ship *Cassandra* in 1720. While he suffered heavy losses, his crew managed to capture the *Cassandra* and secure a haul worth around 75,000 pounds.

It was Edward's leniency towards captives that led to his downfall. He spared the life of *Cassandra*'s captain, James McCrae. His crew saw this as a sign of weakness and marooned him on Mauritius along with three of his loyal men. He survived by scavenging and eventually made his way to the pirate haven Bay of Saint Augustin in Madagascar. There, he lived off the charity of other pirates. He died in late 1720 or early 1721 from some kind of tropical disease.

Chapter 6 – Pirate Ships and Technology

Pirate ships were an essential tool for raiding merchant ships and ports, evading capture, and most especially, navigating the high seas. The choice of ship was imperative. Pirates needed vessels that were fast, maneuverable, and capable of carrying significant amounts of cargo.

Sloops

A sloop is a small vessel that first emerged in the seventeenth century and was a popular choice because of its speed and agility. These ships had a fore-and-aft rigging system that included a single mast with only one main sail and one headsail. This type of rigging made sloops very maneuverable. This was particularly useful for evading larger and more cumbersome naval ships and pursuing merchant vessels. They had a shallow draft that allowed them to sail close to shore and in waters that the larger ships could not venture to. This provided pirates with a tactical advantage when attacking and escaping.

A photograph of a sloop from 1899.[3]

Sloops were used for a variety of purposes besides piracy, including coastal trading. During the eighteenth century, the British Royal Navy used sloops as dispatch vessels and for reconnaissance because of their speed and maneuverability.

Blackbeard used sloops in his early pirating days before capturing larger ships for himself. They were ideal for those quick raids and rapid getaways that he favored and characterized many pirate operations.

Sloops typically carried a crew of up to seventy-five men and were armed with up to a dozen small cannons. Despite their smaller size, they were formidable opponents.

Over time, the design of sloops changed to accommodate longer voyages and larger cargo capacities. The Bermuda sloop became a notable variant. This sloop featured a Bermuda rig with triangular sails that provided better wind efficiency and speed. This improvement made this design incredibly popular.

Today, sloops are popular in recreational sailing and yacht racing because of their versatility and ease of handling. Modern sloops come in various sizes from small day sailors to larger cruising vessels. They are still valued for their speed, agility, and simple rigging.

Schooners

A schooner could have two or three masts with fore-and-aft sails. These vessels were likewise developed in the late seventeenth century by the Dutch before being adapted extensively in North America. The name "schooner" is believed to come from the Dutch word *schoener.* This type of ship became particularly popular in New England during the early eighteenth century.

Schooners featured a hull that was designed for speed and a rigging system that allowed for excellent maneuverability. The foremast was shorter than the mainmast. They used a variety of sales that included a mainsail, foresail, jib, staysail, and topsail. This configuration of sales allowed them to sail close to the wind and made them highly efficient in a variety of wind conditions. Their narrow hulls and shallow drafts allowed them to navigate the coastal waters, making them ideal for both trade and piracy.

Drawing of a schooner.'

Pirates favored schooners because of their speed, agility, and their more moderate cargo capacity. They were bigger than sloops but still agile, which made them suitable for those quick strikes and retreats. They could also carry a significant number of crew members (between sixty and seventy-five). Schooners were armed with around eight to twelve cannons and some swivel guns. Carrying this type of armament made them serious opponents that were capable of intimidating merchant ships into submission.

Both Charles Vane and Blackbeard used schooners for their raids throughout their careers as pirates.

Brigantines

Brigantines were two-masted vessels that combined square-rigged sails on the foremast and fore-and-aft sails on the main mast. This sail combination allowed them to be highly maneuverable and efficient in a variety of wind conditions. They could also navigate shallow waters, which made them an excellent choice for both piracy and privateering.

They were larger than sloops and schooners but smaller than frigates. They ranged from 50 to 200 tons and between lengths of 80 to 100 feet. The foremast was fully square-rigged (the principal sail was at right angles to the length of the ship). The main mast was gaff rigged (the sail had four corners, was fore-and-aft rigged, and controlled at its peak). Their design also included a long mast and a top mast, which made the brigantine suitable for both speed and cargo capacity. They came heavily armed and could carry up to twelve guns.

The term brigantine originally referred to small ships carrying both sails and oars that were used by Mediterranean pirates. Over time, the term changed and described the two-masted sailing vessels that were known for their greater sailing power and agility. They became incredibly popular during the colonial period in the New World, especially in the West Indies.

Pirates favored brigantines for their ability to carry significant amounts of cargo while remaining effective in their raiding and escaping tactics. The combination of speed, firepower, and cargo space made brigantines a versatile ship for a variety of piratical activities. Calico Jack and Anne Bonny often used brigantines for their endeavors.

Brigantines offered advantages over other pirate ships like sloops and schooners since their design allowed them to navigate both the open seas and the shallow coastal waters. Combined with their ability to carry more crew and armaments, this made them more suited for extended battles and long voyages. Pirates tried to plan out long campaigns, so the longer the ship could stay at sea, the better.

Frigates

Frigates were the warships of the Golden Age of Piracy. They were known for their speed, firepower, and versatility despite their size. These were typically medium-sized, three-masted vessels that were equipped with a combination of square and fore-and-aft sails. Frigates were designed for speed and maneuverability, which allowed them to perform well in all sorts of wind conditions.

Frigates were specifically designed for naval warfare and patrolling duties. They usually carried their main battery of cannons on a single deck or on two decks. Additional guns were then mounted on the forecastle and quarterdeck. On average they carried between twenty-four and thirty-eight guns. They were thus well armed and capable of engaging larger ships and defending against smaller, faster vessels.

An example of a frigate from 1802.[5]

Frigates served multiple roles. They were often used as escort ships that protected merchant convoys from pirates and enemy warships.

Their speed also made them useful as scouts and patrol ships. You would find them tasked with reconnaissance and quick response duties.

Frigates were primarily naval vessels. However, their impressive capabilities did not go unnoticed by pirates. Their combination of speed, firepower and cargo capacity allowed pirates to undertake more ambitious raids and fend off naval pursuers more effectively. They were valuable assets for pirates who managed to capture and commandeer them to enhance their own fleets. However, their size and complexity meant they were less commonly used by pirates compared to smaller, more manageable ships.

Notable pirates such as Black Sam Bellamy utilized frigates to great effect. Bellamy's infamous ship, the *Whydah*, was originally a heavily armed frigate before he transformed it into a fearsome pirate vessel.

Galleons

When most people think of the masted sailing ships of the eighteenth century, they picture galleons. These were the large, multi-deck sailing ships developed in the sixteenth century and designed for both warfare and cargo transport.

Galleons were impressive in size. They typically featured three or four masts with a combination of square and lateen sails. They were built with high forecastles and sterncastles that provided a strategic vantage point during battle. Their construction emphasized durability and strength, enabling them to withstand long voyages and rough seas.

Your average galleon could weigh 500 to 1200 tons and measure up to 160 feet in length. These ships were heavily armed and capable of carrying up to sixty cannons.

Galleons were primarily used by European navies and merchants, but their large cargo capacity and formidable firepower did make them attractive targets for pirates. Captains like Captain Kidd and Black Bart Roberts often commanded galleons they had captured. They used their extensive storage space to haul large amounts of loot. The heavy armament also allowed them to dominate smaller pirate ships and merchant vessels.

A Spanish galleon.[5]

The firing capacity and cargo capacity of galleons were advantages, but they were much slower and less maneuverable than sloops and schooners. This made them less than ideal for the quick strike and escape tactics. They compensated for this with their ability to serve as floating fortresses during extended engagements. The sheer presence of a galleon could deter potential attackers and stood as a symbol of power across the seas.

Galleons were a large part of the Spanish treasure fleets. These were known as the Manila galleons. They transported precious goods like silver, gold, silk, and spices between Asia and the Americas. These treasure ships were prime targets for pirates despite their formidable defenses. Still, only four Manila galleons were ever successfully captured by pirates during their 250 years of operation.

Dutch Fluyt

Developed in the sixteenth century in the town of Hoorn, Netherlands, the Dutch fluyt (or fleut) was revolutionary when it came to sailing vessels. It was primarily designed for cargo transport, but it became the cornerstone of Dutch maritime dominance in the seventeenth century.

The fluyt was unique. It had a narrow beam and a bulbous hold that tapered upward toward the deck, a design that maximized cargo space while minimizing the number of crew required to operate the vessel. This significantly reduced operating costs. The typical length-to-beam ratio of these ships ranged from 4:1 to 6:1, and they often featured three masts with square sails on the fore and main masts and a lateen sail on the mizzenmast.

One of the key advantages of this ship was its shallow draft. This allowed it to navigate through shallow waters and ports that were inaccessible to larger ships. It was incredibly suited for trading in the shallow coastal waters of the Baltic Sea and other trading hubs in northern Europe.

The fluyt's design was influenced by economic factors, which included the tolls that were imposed by Denmark for passage through the Øresund strait. These tolls were based on the area of a ship's deck. By having a small deck area relative to its cargo capacity, this ship incurred minimal fees.

Its large cargo capacity made it the preferred vessel for transporting bulk goods like grain, timber, and other commodities. This did not make it suitable for conversion to a warship, unlike the other vessels of the time, but allowed it to carry twice the cargo of similarly sized ships designed for dual purposes. Obviously, with this large cargo hold and efficient design, it was an attractive target for pirates. The ship's ability to carry substantial quantities of loot made it a valuable prize. Some pirates even managed to capture and use them for their own purposes.

Pirate Weaponry

Cannons

The pirates of the golden age used cannons to disable and intimidate their target ships from a distance. These cannons could vary in size and were typically used to fire cannonballs that weighed between 3.5 and 5.5 kilograms. Other types of ammunition included chain shot—two half-balls connected by a chain—which was used to destroy masts and rigging. There was also grapeshot, which scattered small metal balls to maim crew members and damage sails.

Pistols

Pirates would often carry multiple flintlock pistols due to their slow reloading time. They were short range weapons only effective for a few yards. Often, you'd find pirates using pistols that were elaborately decorated to display their status and wealth. Blackbeard was known to carry several pistols at once to make quick, successive shots.

Cutlasses

The cutlass was a short, broad saber that held a single sharp edge. It also had a protective hand guard to protect the user in close combat. It was a versatile tool and could be used for tasks on land and at sea, much like a machete. The cutlass was favored by pirates for its effectiveness in the cramped and chaotic conditions of shipboard fights.

Muskets

For longer range engagements, pirates used the musket. However, much like pistols, they had a slow reload time, so they were less favored for immediate combat situations. Pirates would often saw off the barrels and stocks to make muskets easier to handle in close quarters. The flintlock mechanism replaced the earlier matchlock and provided more reliable firing in wet conditions.

Blunderbuss

This was a short, large-bore gun that could be loaded with a variety of projectiles. Many used nails and glass to scatter over a wide area. It was an effective defense against boarding enemies because of its wide shot pattern and devastating impact.

Boarding Axes and Grappling Hooks

Boarding axes were used to cut through rigging and climb aboard enemy ships. Grappling hooks helped pirates latch onto and pull in vessels for boarding purposes. These tools were needed for taking over enemy ships and the ensuing close-quarter combat.

Pirate Tactics

Boarding

Boarding was the primary tactic used by pirates. They pulled alongside a target ship and used grappling hooks to pull the ship closer and then board with weapons like cutlasses and pistols. The chaos and close-quarter nature of boarding favored the pirates.

Surprise Attacks

The element of surprise is a pirate's favorite weapon. They used false flags or hid under their armament so they could get close to their target ship before revealing their true intentions. This particular tactic minimized the chance of resistance and damage to their own ships.

Intimidation

Intimidation was also one of their favorite tactics. They used intimidation to force merchant ships to surrender. This included flying the infamous Jolly Roger—a black flag with skulls and crossbones that signaled that no mercy would be given if resistance was encountered. The psychological impact of the pirate reputation often led to quick surrenders without a fight.

Chapter 7 – Pirate Culture and Society

The life of a pirate has been heavily romanticized. The reality is that it was structured and harsh. Pirates had to adhere to a strict schedule to maintain discipline and efficiency. Their day typically began at sunrise with attending to various ship duties like repairing sails, scrubbing decks, and maintaining their weapons. Regular watches were established to make sure that the ship was constantly monitored for any threats or potential targets. They operated in shifts: some crew members rested while others worked.

Food aboard ship was basic and strictly aimed at keeping the crew alive. They weren't trying to satisfy any culinary desires. Common staples included hardtack, salted meat, and dried beans. Occasionally, they'd acquire fresh fruits and vegetables. Fresh water was precious. It was often stored in barrels and rationed out very carefully. Pirates also consumed a lot of alcohol in the form of rum and beer as it was safer to drink alcohol than the often-contaminated water. The alcoholic beverages also played a big role in their pirate culture and served as a form of sustenance and leisure.

Life at sea was stressful and often very monotonous. Pirates were very good at finding ways to entertain themselves. Singing sea shanties, gambling, and storytelling were popular pastimes. But they also spent a significant amount of their time planning and preparing for their next raid, which involved serious strategizing and maintaining their weapons and ship.

Pirate Code

Pirates have a lawless reputation, but they operated under a democratic system. Pirate ships had a set of rules often called the pirate code or articles. All crew members had to agree to and abide by these rules, which covered everything from the distribution of loot to punishments for breaking the law.

Democratic Decision-Making

Every member had a vote in important decisions. This included electing a captain and other officers, deciding on battle strategies, and dividing loot. The captain held significant power during times of battle but was otherwise subject to the crew's decisions. The system of checks and balances help prevent anyone individual from wielding too much power over the others. Pirate captains were often elected based on their leadership and navigational skills. Their authority could be revoked if the crew was dissatisfied with their command. This egalitarian approach made sure that loyalty was emphasized and minimized the risk of mutiny.

Distribution of Loot

Pirate codes meticulously outlined how any loot was to be divided among the crew. Often, the captain and quartermaster received larger shares, reflective of their leadership roles and responsibilities. Other officers would receive slightly more than regular crew members. The distribution was designed to be fair and motivate the entire crew.

Compensation for Injuries

The pirates' profession was dangerous, and they recognized this. They provided compensation for injuries sustained in the line of duty. Specific amounts were allocated for the loss of limbs, eyes, or other severe injuries. A common fund collected from their plunder was used to payout for injuries. This early form of insurance made sure that injured pirates and their families were cared for. It promoted a sense of security and camaraderie with the crew. Pirates were really ahead of their time!

The amounts of compensation changed depending on the ship and captain, but they were always substantial:

- **Bartholomew "Black Bart" Roberts' Code:** Provided 600 pieces of eight for the loss of an arm, 400 pieces of eight for the loss of a leg, and 100 pieces of eight for the loss of an eye.

- **John Phillips' Code:** Allocated 600 pieces of eight or six slaves for the loss of a right arm and slightly less for other limbs.

- **Edward Low and George Lowther's Code:** Offered up to 800 pieces of eight for the loss of an arm or leg, with additional compensation for permanent disfigurement.

Behavior and Discipline

Maintaining order aboard a pirate ship required strict discipline. There were punishments for offenses like theft, fighting, or neglecting duties, and they were severe. Pirates had to keep their weapons clean and ready for battle, avoid unnecessary violence on board, and follow rules around curfew and gambling to maintain order and efficiency. Punishments often included flogging, marooning, or even execution for serious crimes like murder. For lesser infractions, pirates could receive reduced shares of loot or temporary demotions. The crew typically decided the punishment collectively to prevent the abuse of power by any individual. Despite the harsh penalties, the system maintained a semblance of order and fairness within the pirate community that was highly attractive.

Here are descriptions of some of the harshest punishments:

- **Marooning:** Offenders were left on a deserted island with minimal supplies, a severe form of punishment for serious crimes like theft or desertion.

- **Flogging:** Whipping with a cat-o'-nine-tails was a common punishment for lesser offenses. This public display served as a deterrent to others.

- **Keelhauling:** In severe cases, offenders were dragged under the ship's keel, a brutal punishment that often resulted in severe injury or death.

- **Nose and Ear Slitting:** For theft among crew members, a common punishment was slitting the nose and ears before marooning the offender. This not only punished the individual but also marked them as criminals to others.

Progressive Pirates

Pirate crews were quite progressive for their time. They often disregarded race and nationality. Many of the pirates were former sailors or marginalized individuals who wanted a different way of life away from the harsh conditions of the Navy or merchant ships. Freed slaves and people from all different backgrounds could find a place among pirates, who valued skill and loyalty over social status and skin color.

Governance and Structure

As mentioned, captains only truly had power during engagements. Outside of combat, they had little say and had to respect the wishes of the crew. The quartermaster acted as a counterbalance to the captain's power. He handled the distribution of loot, enforced the pirate code, and represented the crew's interests. This was yet another arrangement that made sure that the power was not concentrated on a single individual and that the crew had a voice in everything.

Symbols and Mythology

Pirate Flags

The most iconic symbol of piracy was the Jolly Roger. As mentioned earlier, this was a black flag featuring a skull and crossbones designed to instill fear and signal that no mercy would be given to anyone who resisted. The use of the skull and crossbones symbol on pirate flags dates to the late seventeenth century. It was possibly influenced by the Barbary pirate's designs. Emmanuel Wynn, a French pirate, is often credited with the first use of the Jolly Roger in 1700. His flag featured a skull, crossbones, and an hourglass.

The origins of the term "Jolly Roger" are highly debated. One theory suggests it came from the French phrase *Joli Rouge*, meaning "Pretty Red." This refers to the red flags that were initially flown by pirates to show no quarter. Another theory states that it comes from the English term "Old Roger," which was a nickname for the devil. This idea says it reflects the pirates' ruthless nature.

One of two pirate flags considered to be authentic.[7]

Beyond the Jolly Roger, pirates customized their flags to convey specific messages. Blackbeard's flag depicted a skeleton holding an hourglass and a spear, with a bleeding heart. This symbolized imminent death for any who defied him. Calico Jack Rackham's flag featured a skull with crossed cutlasses to emphasize his readiness for combat. Bartholomew Roberts, known as Black Bart, had a flag showing a pirate standing on two skulls. One skull was labeled "ABH" and to the other "AMH." This stood for "a Barbadian head" and "a Martinican head" to symbolize his victories over his enemies.

Pirates used flags as a type of psychological warfare. They were designed to strike terror into the hearts of sailors and often led to quick surrenders. The sighting of a Jolly Roger showed that a pirate crew was near and often led merchant ships to surrender without a bite to avoid a brutal confrontation. It was a great tactic that minimized resistance and reduced the risk of damage to both ships and crew.

The pirates would initially approach their targets under false or friendly flags just to get close and only reveal their true colors when they were close enough to attack. This created panic and confusion in their victims. These flags made piracy more efficient and profitable.

Superstitions

Sailors in general were deeply superstitious, and pirates were no different. They adhered to a variety of rituals and beliefs to avoid misfortune and make sure their survival odds were greater on the unpredictable seas. These superstitions were a blend of maritime traditions and pirate-specific lore.

It was widely believed that whistling on board ship could whistle up a storm. Anyone who whistled on ship was blamed for bringing bad weather and dangerous conditions. This belief stemmed from the fear that whistling would offend the wind gods and lead to adverse weather conditions.

Having bananas on board a ship was considered bad luck. It's believed this superstition was caused by bananas releasing ethylene gas. This caused other fruits to ripen and spoil faster. The rapid decomposition of bananas would also attract pests and contribute to accidents and ship disappearances.

Killing an albatross was believed to bring severe bad luck. Albatross birds were thought to carry the souls of deceased sailors. On the other hand, seeing an albatross was a good omen and symbolized the presence of a guiding spirit.

Cats, especially black ones, were considered good luck on ships. They controlled the rodent population and were believed to protect the sailors from harm. Polydactyl cats (cats with extra toes) were highly valued for their superior climbing and hunting abilities.

A shark found following the ship was seen as a sign that someone on board would die soon. Pirates believed that sharks sensed impending death and followed the ships to feed on the bodies of the deceased.

Dolphins swimming alongside the ship were considered good luck. They were seen as protectors, and they ensured a safe voyage.

Myths and Legends

Pirates regularly told myths and stories as part of the effort to relieve boredom. The myth of buried treasures that were popularized by stories like *Treasure Island* suggest that pirates often buried their loot on deserted islands. It's a captivating story full of excitement and maps with an *X* marking the spot. In reality, very few pirates buried their treasure, as most prefer to spend their wealth quickly. The fast and loose lifestyle of pirates left little reason for any long-term treasure hoarding.

Ghost ships, like the *Flying Dutchman*, are central to pirate mythology. The *Flying Dutchman* is a legendary phantom ship that was doomed to sail the oceans forever, never to make port. This was a legend that probably originated in the seventeenth century. It is thought to have originated with the tales of a Dutch captain named Bernard Fokke. He was said to have made a pact with the devil to achieve unprecedented speeds.

According to the myth, the *Flying Dutchman* appears as an omen of doom during stormy weather. The ghost ship serves as a cautionary tale about the perils of the sea and the consequences of trying to defy nature.

Davy Jones' Locker was a term that referred to the ocean's bottom. This was considered the final resting place of drowned sailors and sunken ships. The term dates to at least the eighteenth century and has been popularized through literary works. Davy Jones is often depicted as an evil spirit or devil of the sea. He presides over the depths and welcomes sailors to their watery graves. The exact origin of this myth is unclear. Theories range from a historical pirate named David Jones to folklore that involves the devil and evil spirits. Over time, Davy Jones' Locker has come to symbolize death and the unknown dangers lurking beneath the ocean's surface.

Ship Life and Maintenance

Pirate life was challenging and required significant means to keep the ships operational and manage long voyages efficiently. Maintaining the ship and managing provisions were key parts of survival and success in piracy or any other maritime activities.

Pirate ships underwent constant wear and tear. This came from battles, weather, and the regular issues of sailing. These ships were made from wood, after all. The crew was responsible for several continuous maintenance tasks, completed during their downtime or between battles and engagements. Different crew members were assigned the task of repairing sails, fixing leaks, and reinforcing the hull. Sails often needed mending. Strong winds and storms could tear them, and grapeshot and cannon fire from merchant ships could put holes in them. Pirates used tar and pitch to seal any cracks in the ship's wooden planks. This was necessary; otherwise, water would seep in and cause rot.

Another common practice at the time was careening. The pirates would beach their vessel to clean and repair the hull. The ship would be tilted on its side to remove any barnacles, algae, and other marine growth that slowed the ship down. Careening was also used for more extensive repairs to the ship's underside. Sometimes when the seas were rough, a ship could take a cannonball below the normal water level. While careening, the crew would take advantage of the time ashore to replenish their supplies and find fresh water.

Pirates relied on essential navigation tools, much like other mariners. These tools included compasses, astrolabes, and sextants to chart their courses. It was even more important for pirates to have accurate navigation because they needed to avoid naval patrols, find safe harbors, and locate their potential targets. A well-maintained set of navigation instruments was just as important as the ship's physical condition.

Long Voyages

Not all pirates led small raids from their safe harbors. There were many that went on long voyages, capturing several ships. Pirates would often raid coastal settlements or capture merchant ships to replenish their supplies on long voyages. The ship's cook played a vital role in rationing all the food stuffs and making sure meals were prepared to sustain the crew over long periods of time at sea.

As mentioned, freshwater was prone to contamination. To fight this, pirates would often stop at islands or coastal areas to refill their water supply from natural springs or rivers. If it rained heavily enough at sea, they would also collect rainwater onboard the ship. Maintaining a fresh supply of water was a constant concern as dehydration and the related illnesses could decimate a crew.

The dangers of life at sea weren't always about combat and accidents. There were significant health risks, including scurvy, which was a disease caused by a vitamin C deficiency. Pirates combated scurvy by incorporating any available fresh fruits and vegetables into their diet. Hygiene on ship was minimal, and the cramped and unsanitary conditions often led to outbreaks of disease. This was a challenge. But, as mentioned, pirates developed their own healthcare systems, and their injured crew compensation include disease. They also provided rudimentary medical care, and medicines were a plunder as valuable as gold.

Chapter 8 – The Decline of Piracy

As the eighteenth century progressed, governments, particularly those of Britain, Spain, and France, recognized that piracy posed a significant threat to their maritime trade and colonial interests. They no longer wished to have privateers turning pirate. The response by these powers was a combination of legal reforms, military action, and strategic alliances that were aimed at eradicating piracy entirely. They cracked down hard on these outlaws from the very late seventeenth century through the eighteenth century.

The Piracy Act of 1698 and Other Legal Reforms

The British in particular established legal frameworks and enhanced their naval operations to suppress these criminal activities. One of the most important measures in this campaign was the implementation of the Piracy Act of 1698. This was followed with other legal reforms and military actions that were aimed directly at curbing the pirate menace.

The Piracy Act of 1698

This code, which was enacted under the reign of King William III, was formally known as the "Act for the More Effectual Suppression of Piracy." It addressed the growing threat of piracy but providing a comprehensive legal framework in order to prosecute pirates more effectively. The following are some of the key provisions of the act.

Establishment of Admiralty Courts

The act established admiralty courts in the colonies, which were given the power to try pirates swiftly and efficiently. This helped ensure that justice was administered without the delays typically associated with sending pirates back to England for their trial. The admiralty courts operated under a more streamlined and less formal procedure compared to the more familiar common law courts. This made trials and sentences quicker. It was designed to maintain Britain's momentum against piracy and knock them out as fast as possible.

Legal Procedures and Penalties

The act also detailed very specific legal procedures for the prosecution of pirates. This included the collection and presentation of evidence, the roles of witnesses, and the rights of the accused to present a defense. Severe penalties were created for convicted pirates, including death by hanging. The public execution of pirates was designed to serve as a powerful deterrent and a clear message to anyone who might think about becoming a pirate. They wanted everyone to be aware of the risks involved in piracy. Piracy had been an appealing lifestyle previously because of the gray area of privateering. But by the late seventeenth century, pirates were strictly considered criminals and outlaws. The times had changed, and there were no more legal pirates.

Proclamation for Suppressing of Pirates (1717)

Building on the Piracy Act of 1698, the British Crown issued the Proclamation for Suppressing of Pirates in 1717. This proclamation offered another option for pirates. The British Crown decided to provide an opportunity for pirates to abandon their criminal activities without facing execution. Those who surrendered within a certain period were offered royal pardons. It was an interesting way to tackle the issue. At the same time, there was language included for those who were tempted to reject this pardon opportunity. The proclamation delineated severe consequences for those who continued their activities after the established amount of time. This created a legal and psychological pressure on pirates to give up their way of life.

Increased Naval Presence

These legal reforms and royal pardons were amplified by an increased naval presence. The British Royal Navy ramped up its efforts to patrol pirate-infested waters and found notable success in eradicating piracy.

One of the most famous naval engagements against pirates was the previously-related capture of Edward Teach (Blackbeard) by Lieutenant Robert Maynard of the Royal Navy in 1718 at Ocracoke Island, North Carolina. Another of the Royal Navy's great victories was the siege of Nassau by Governor Woodes Rogers, also in 1718. Rogers' efforts transformed Nassau from a pirate stronghold into a lawful colony and significantly reduced pirate activities in the region. Much like Nassau, Tortuga and Port Royal were subjected to naval campaigns that disrupted their roles as pirate hubs.

Black Bart, or Bartholomew Roberts, was one of the most successful pirates of this era. He is said to have captured over 400 ships. However, his success came to an end in 1722. Captain Chaloner Ogle of the HMS *Swallow* attacked Roberts off the coast of West Africa. In a fierce battle, Roberts was killed, and his crew was captured. Roberts had been one of the last major pirate leaders still active, so this was a significant blow to piracy.

Between these campaigns against significant pirates and the increased patrols in key areas known for pirate activities, the lives of pirates were seriously impacted. The Caribbean, the American coastline, and the West African coast were all inundated with naval ships, especially those belonging to the British Royal Navy. Warships were stationed strategically to intercept pirate vessels and protect the merchant shipping lanes. The presence of these warships acted as an incredible deterrent and made it far more difficult for pirates to operate freely. The European powers had declared war on piracy.

While the British Navy may have been the most present power, international cooperation played a key role in suppressing piracy. The European powers created treaties and agreements to facilitate coordinated naval patrols and shared intelligence on pirate movements. It was this cooperation that helped ensure that pirates had fewer places to hide.

Key Naval Stations

In the Caribbean, the British set up a strong naval presence with bases in Jamaica, Barbados, and the Leeward Islands. These bases served as launch points for all their anti-piracy patrols and provided logistical support for any naval operations in the area.

Along the American coastline, they set up bases in areas like Chesapeake Bay and the Carolinas, where pirates had frequently raided merchant ships. This military presence led to the capture of pirates like Stede Bonnet in South Carolina.

Economic Measures

Many governments also started implementing economic measures that were designed to undermine the foundations of pirate operations.

The governments recognized that the pirates depended on black markets to sell their stolen goods. To disrupt these networks, they increased surveillance of ports that were known for illegal activities. The authorities set up groups to conduct raids on known pirate-friendly markets and confiscated goods, and this led to the arrest of traders who dealt with pirates. By tightening their control over these markets, the governments effectively cut off a significant revenue stream for pirates. It became more and more difficult for pirates to profit from their activities, making their lifestyle senseless.

Governments also started to enforce trade regulations. Colonial administrations were ordered to implement and enforce trade laws far more rigorously than they had in the past. Ships and cargo were to be inspected more frequently to prevent the transport of stolen goods. These regulations help make it riskier and less profitable for merchants to trade with pirates, further isolating pirate networks.

The government also started offering incentives for legal trading activities. It became more profitable to follow the rules and not collaborate with pirates. Tax breaks, subsidies, and protection from naval convoys were provided to merchants who adhered to legal trade practices. The idea was to encourage legitimate commerce while undermining the appeal of piracy.

Impact of Anti-Pirate Measures

This combined attack on the military, legal, and economic front led to a significant decline in the number of active pirates. The increased naval presence made it far more difficult for pirates to operate with impunity. Numerous pirates accepted the legal pardons, while those who didn't were captured and killed in naval engagements. And the destruction of pirate havens like Nassau, Tortuga, and Port Royal deprived the pirates of a safe place to repair their ships, resupply, and plan their raids.

These aggressive antipiracy campaigns also had a psychological impact and anyone who was considering becoming a pirate. The threat of severe punishment, which included public executions and the display of captured pirates' dead bodies, served as a very powerful deterrent. The infamous executions of pirate captains like William Kidd and Stede Bonnet highlighted all the risks associated with being a pirate and discouraged new recruits.

Famous Trials and Executions

While we've mentioned some of these trials and executions in passing, the following section takes a closer look at a few of the most infamous cases.

The Case of Captain Kidd

Captain William Kidd's trial and execution is one of the most famous cases in history. His trial began on May 8, 1701, at the Old Bailey in London. If you recall, he was charged with piracy and the murder of his gunner, William Moore. The trial was highly publicized and controversial. There were many debates over the fairness of the proceedings. Despite his defense, which in all honesty was a good one, he was found guilty on all charges. On May 23, 1701, he was hanged at Execution Dock in Wapping, London. The first attempt to complete his execution was botched. The rope broke, and he had to be hanged a second time. His body was then tarred and hung in a gibbet on the River Thames.

Kidd's trial and execution had a significant cultural and psychological impact. It was one of the first and served as a stark warning to other pirates and potential recruits. His execution was made a public spectacle. Combine this with the gruesome display of his body, and it underscored the severe consequences of piracy. It showed everyone that the world was changing, and that piracy was not a legitimate occupation anymore.

The Charleston Pirate Trials of 1718

The Charleston pirate trials of 1718 were an important moment in the battle against piracy in the early eighteenth century. These trials included the prosecution of the infamous Stede Bonnet, the "Gentleman Pirate."

The thirteen separate trials began on October 28, 1718, at the house of Garrett Vanvelsen and continued for three weeks. Judge Nicholas Trott presided over these proceedings, in which a total of fifty-eight men were accused of piracy. The courtroom was small, so the defendants were tried in smaller groups. Of the fifty-eight men, forty-nine were convicted and sentenced to death.

Judge Trott was under significant scrutiny from British authorities and meticulously prepared for these trials. He made sure that all legal procedures were followed to the tiniest extent. The trials lacked any defense attorneys. The accused had to defend themselves, which from a modern standpoint is a gross injustice. Many of the accused unsuccessfully tried to defend themselves against the charges brought by Attorney General Richard Allein and his assistant Thomas Hepworth.

Stede Bonnet's trial was a significant highlight. Bonnet was brought to trial separately from his crew. Despite his personal defense and request for clemency, Bonnet was found guilty of piracy and hanged at White Point (now White Point Garden) on December 10, 1718. Twenty-nine members of his crew were executed almost a month earlier.

This heavily publicized series of trials was a turning point in the fight against piracy. They were made a major spectacle because piracy had become a major threat to colonial trade and security. Their aim was to demonstrate the severe consequences of piracy no matter who you were. These trials were a legal process but also a psychological campaign to instill fear and deter future would-be pirates from taking up this life. They showcased the determination of the colonial authorities to restore order and protect commerce. These trials were meticulously documented, and combined with the public executions, underscored the seriousness with which piracy was addressed during this era.

Other Factors Leading to the Decline of Piracy

It wasn't that the colonizing powers and governments suddenly decided to crack down on piracy. It was more complicated than that. Colonial governments began consolidating and strengthening themselves, which played a significant role in combating piracy. European powers like Britain, France, and Spain wanted to expand their colonial territories, so they established a stronger administrative and military presence in their colonies. This increased their ability to enforce their anti-piracy laws and conduct military operations against the pirate strongholds. In essence, the colonial governments became more organized and invested in their colonies.

The Treaty of Utrecht in 1713 ended the Spanish War of Succession. This included provisions for cooperation between European powers to combat piracy, spurring coordinated naval patrols and joint efforts to eradicate the pirate bases in the eighteenth century. These nations deciding to collaborate made it harder for pirates to find safe havens and sell their plundered goods.

Beyond the previously mentioned governance and legal reforms, certain technological advancements made it much easier to combat piracy. The eighteenth century witnessed significant advancements in naval technology. Ships became faster, more maneuverable, and better armed. The development of more effective naval artillery and the improvement of shipbuilding techniques allowed navies to better patrol pirate-infested waters and engage pirate ships. These advancements made it increasingly more difficult for pirates to escape.

There was also improved communication between naval vessels and colonial administrations. They were able to share intelligence about pirate movements and coordinate responses to pirate threats. This greatly enhanced the effectiveness of anti-piracy operations and made it harder for pirates to operate undetected.

It also helped that the public sentiment toward piracy had shifted. The media coverage of pirate trials and executions increased, publicizing sensational accounts of pirate exploits and the brutal punishments that were meted out to captured pirates. This reinforced the dangers of choosing the pirate's life and discouraged many from joining their ranks, helping to de-romanticize the idea of piracy.

As the European colonies became more established, opportunities for legitimate work also increased. This stabilization of the colonial economies and the availability of legal employment reduced the allure of piracy for many. There were more stable and profitable alternatives, so fewer people were tempted to turn to piracy.

Chapter 9 – Piracy in the Mediterranean and Asia

While the Caribbean in the Americas took center stage in all the popular accounts from the Golden Age of Piracy, piracy was also rampant in the Mediterranean and Asian waters. We've touched on this briefly but now we'll go into more detail.

Barbary Corsairs

The Barbary corsairs, also known simply as the Barbary pirates, were an intimidating group of seafaring marauders who had a major impact on Mediterranean trade and politics. The peak of their activity spanned from the early sixteenth century into the early nineteenth century.

Their rise in the late fifteenth and early sixteenth centuries coincided with the expansion of the Ottoman Empire into the western Mediterranean. They started off as an extension of the Ottoman naval power, receiving support and protection from the empire. This arrangement, much like that of privateers, allowed them to disrupt European shipping and conduct raids on coastal towns with relative freedom.

The corsairs operated from well-fortified ports all along the North African coast, including Algiers, Tunis, Tripoli, and Rabat. These were cities that were nominally under Ottoman control. Operationally, they were independent and run by local leaders who often came to power through force or election by the local military elite.

The corsairs themselves were a hierarchical society organized into highly efficient and brutal raiding parties. At the top were the deys, beys, or pashas. They oversaw the strategic direction of the society. The raiding parties were led by seasoned captains known as reis.

Like other pirates, they used fast and agile galleys to carry out their attacks. The primary target of these pirates were European merchant ships and coastal settlements. They were known for their swift and brutal attacks, which often resulted in the capture of valuable goods and the enslavement of local populations.

These raids were devastating for the coastal communities. Towns and villages were frequently abandoned as the residents fled inland to escape the threat of enslavement. The economic toll on European maritime trade was significant. As a result, many of the nations decided to take measures to protect their shipping and their coasts.

Infamous Figures

The Barbarossa Brothers: Oruç and Hayreddin

Oruç Barbarossa (1474-1518)

Oruç Barbarossa, also known as Baba Oruç, happens to be one of the most notorious Barbary corsairs. He was born on the island of Lesbos to a Turkish father and a Greek mother. He began his career by attacking Aegean ships. Eventually, he was taken captive but then freed by Egyptian forces. After obtaining this freedom, he started working with his brother Hayreddin out of the port of Alexandria, using ships that were provided by the local ruler.

Around 1505, Oruç moved his operations to the western Mediterranean, establishing a base in Djerba. His fame only grew. He seized numerous merchant and warships, particularly Spanish vessels, and was instrumental in driving the Spanish out of Algiers in 1516. After this accomplishment, he declared himself Sultan of Algiers. His rule was short-lived as he was killed by the Spanish in 1518 while defending the city of Tlemcen. However, his leadership laid the groundwork for his brother to expand their influence even further.

Hayreddin Barbarossa (c. 1478-1546)

Following the death of his brother, Hayreddin (Khizr) took over their little empire and continued his brother's ambitions to solidify and expand their power base. He was known for his tactical genius and fierce naval capabilities. Their efforts successfully made Algiers a significant hub for piracy. Hayreddin captured the strategic Peñón of Algiers in 1529 from the Spanish.

In 1533, Suleiman the Magnificent appointed Hayreddin as Kapudan Pasha (Grand Admiral) of the Ottoman Navy. His most notable military achievement was his victory at the Battle of Preveza in 1538. With this victory, he secured Ottoman naval dominance in the Mediterranean. He also led campaigns in Tunis and cooperated with the French against the Spanish. Hayreddin retired to Istanbul in 1545 and died the following year.

Turgut Reis (1485-1565)

Turgut Reis was also known as Dragut Reis. He began his career under Hayreddin and quickly gained a reputation for daring raids and strategy. He expanded the corsairs' activities into the central Mediterranean and even threatened the coasts of Italy and Spain. He helped with the Ottoman naval victories and was later appointed the governor of Tripoli, which he turned into a major base for corsair operations. His strategic mind and relentless raids solidified his reputation as one of the most feared corsairs of his time.

Murat Reis the Elder

Murat Reis the Elder was known for his naval expertise and bold expeditions. He extended Barbary corsair activities into the Atlantic, reaching as far as Iceland and the Azores. He captured many ships and conducted raids on distant European coasts, enhancing the fearsome reputation of the Barbary corsairs.

Economic and Political Impact

The Barbary States operated with a certain degree of freedom, but their activities indirectly supported the Ottoman Empire. They were an integral part of bolstering the empire's wealth and influence.

Piracy was central to the economy of the Barbary States. The corsairs' activities weren't just about plunder but were highly organized and financed by wealthy backers who shared in their profits. These investors provided the resources the pirates needed, like ships and weapons, and expected a portion of the loot in return. This economic model supported a significant part of the local economy, enriching both corsairs and their backers.

One of the primary sources of revenue was the capture and sale of tens of thousands of European slaves. These captives were sold in the extensive slave markets of North Africa and the Ottoman Empire, which were integrated into the broader economic framework of the region. The demand for slaves was high. These markets were well organized and made slavery a lucrative business for the corsairs. Many of these captives were ransomed back to their families for large sums of money.

The Barbary corsairs had a much more significant influence than average pirates. They were a huge part of regional conflicts but also the balance of power in the Mediterranean, playing a vital role in the Ottoman Empire's strategy to counter the European powers. They had an active part in assisting the Ottomans against the Knights of Saint John, which culminated in the capture of Rhodes in 1522. This victory removed a significant Christian stronghold in the Mediterranean and secured Ottoman dominance in the region.

However, the corsairs also engaged in alliances and conflicts with European states. The constant threat posed by the Barbary corsairs forced European nations to invest heavily in their naval defenses and diplomatic efforts. They had to work harder to secure their shipping routes. This constant conflict helped contribute to the development of stronger navies and more sophisticated maritime strategies. They helped shape the political landscape of the Mediterranean as well as the Caribbean and Americas.

The Decline of the Corsairs

By the late seventeenth century, the power of the Barbary corsairs started to wane.

The European nations joined together to implement more effective naval strategies against piracy. These strategies included the deployment of stronger, faster ships and better organized fleets. These could easily counter the corsairs' swift and unpredictable raids. European powers also started to strike back at the Barbary States much like they did in the Caribbean in the Americas. This made it much more difficult for the corsairs to operate freely, compelling them to make peace and cease attacks on shipping.

Still, the Barbary corsairs remained a persistent threat throughout the eighteenth century. European coastal towns and shipping routes continued to suffer from their raids, if in smaller amounts. This prompted more rigorous military campaigns. The turning point for the Barbary corsairs came with the intervention of the United States and other European nations early in the nineteenth century. This led to the

The Barbary Wars

The First Barbary War from 1801 to 1805 and the Second Barbary War in 1815 were key events that reduced the power of the corsairs. The wars were started by the United States in response to the constant pirate attacks and demands for tribute. The US Navy, along with naval forces from Sweden and the Kingdom of Sicily, engaged in military actions to protect their shipping and reduce the threat from the Barbary States. Both wars saw significant naval engagements that included blockades and bombardments of pirate strongholds. The success of the military actions forced the Barbary States to sign treaties that seriously curtailed their piratical activities. These treaties also included demands for the release of captured American and European sailors.

French Conquest of Algiers

The final blow to the Barbary corsairs came with the French conquest of Algiers in 1830. This invasion was part of a broader strategy to establish colonial control over North Africa. The French also wanted to eliminate the corsair threat once and for all. The capture of Algiers marked the end of significant pirate activity in the region. The French established a colonial administration that suppressed any remaining pirate operations.

Asian Piracy

The Indian Ocean and Southeast Asia have long reigned as regions of significant maritime activity shaped by trade, cultural exchanges, and piracy. The waters there have served as critical maritime routes connecting the East and the West, facilitating the movement of goods, people, and ideas across vast distances.

The Indian Ocean stretches from the eastern coast of Africa to the western shores of Australia and encompasses the Arabian Sea, the Bay of Bengal, and the Andaman Sea. Southeast Asia has a myriad of islands and peninsulas that include present-day Indonesia, Malaysia, the Philippines, and Thailand. It features a complex network of narrow straits and broad seas like the Strait of Malacca and the South China Sea.

This region was a melting pot of many cultures and civilizations that were driven by extensive maritime trade. Major trading centers like Calicut, Malacca, and Guangzhou thrived on the exchange of spices, silk, precious metals, and other valuable commodities. The area was known for its economic prosperity, and this attracted traders from the Arab world, Persia, India, China, and later, Europe. This wealth also drew the attention of pirates who thought to capitalize on the lucrative trade routes throughout this area.

Like many other seaways, the Indian Ocean and Southeast Asia have a history of piracy dating back to ancient times. Early records indicate the presence of sea raiders and corsairs. Indigenous pirate groups operated along the coasts and inlets and took advantage of their intimate knowledge of the local waters. The earliest pirates engaged in raiding coastal settlements and ambushing merchant vessels. Much like other pirates, they disrupted trade and caused considerable instability.

One of the more notable pirate groups was the Lanun, or Illanun, pirates of the Philippines. They terrorized the Sulu Sea and beyond from the seventeenth to the nineteenth centuries. They were known for their fast prahu boats and ruthless tactics of capturing slaves and plundering villages.

The Golden Age of Asian Piracy

The Golden Age of Piracy in Asia started a bit later than in the Caribbean. It coincided with significant political and economic changes in the region, including the decline of powerful empires, such as the Ming dynasty in China and the Majapahit Empire in Indonesia. This decline created power vacuums that were exploited by pirate leaders. Another factor was European colonial expansion, which brought new opportunities and conflicts that the pirates could exploit.

Among the most infamous pirates of this area was Zheng Yi Sao (also known as Ching Shih). She was born in Guangdong in 1775 and rose to prominence after taking over her husband's fleet in 1807.

Zheng Yi Sao had strict codes of conduct and demonstrated a remarkable strategical mind. Her code prohibited unauthorized attacks, ensured the fair distribution of loot, and set severe punishments for disobedience. Her rules included harsh penalties for crimes like desertion and the mistreatment of women. This code contributed to the high level of organization and loyalty among her pirates.

Under her command, the Red Flag Fleet, consisting of over 70,000 pirates and 1,800 ships, dominated the South China Sea. They conducted many successful raids and defeated multiple Chinese naval fleets. They went to battle against the Chinese Navy in 1808 and 1809. She employed some innovative tactics to overcome these more superior forces. Her fleet's activities disrupted trade severely and instilled fear in both the Chinese and European naval powers operating in the region.

By 1810, she was facing increasing pressures from more coordinated Chinese and European naval forces. She intelligently decided to negotiate a surrender. Her formidable reputation held quite a bit of leverage, enabling her to secure a pardon from the Qing authorities. Her terms were quite favorable. She retained a portion of her fleet and her amassed wealth. After retiring from privacy, she transitioned into a profitable career in smuggling and later opened a gambling house. She lived her remaining years in peace until she died in 1844 at the age of sixty-nine.

European Colonial Impact

The arrival of European colonial powers like the Portuguese, Dutch, and British significantly changed the maritime world in the Indian Ocean in Southeast Asia. These colonial powers strived to dominate the lucrative spice trade and established their own control over key maritime routes. The Portuguese were among the first to arrive and established a foothold in the early sixteenth century by taking strategic ports like Malacca in 1511. They used their naval superiority to seize the indigenous merchant vessels and enforce trading licenses, known as cartazes.

The European powers also introduced the concept of privateering. These privateers, as always, blurred the line between legitimate naval warfare and outright piracy. Like other privateers, when their commissions ended, they often turned to piracy and exacerbated the instability of the region. This was particularly evident with the English and Dutch privateers.

The competition among European colonial powers led to constant conflicts and shifting alliances, further complicating the dynamics in the region. During the Napoleonic Wars, the British temporarily took control of Dutch territories in Southeast Asia. This era saw increased naval activity as colonial powers tried to secure their own interests and often resorted to piracy or privateering to take down their rivals. The British established Singapore in 1819 as a key trading post, and this was a strategic move to counter Dutch influence in the region.

Suppression of Asian Piracy

Much like a century before in the Caribbean and Americas, by the nineteenth century, coordinated military efforts and colonial administrations started to effectively combat piracy. They also created legal frameworks to prosecute pirates, which further reduced the number of people turning to piracy.

The British, Dutch, and Portuguese created maritime defenses and naval bases in strategic locations like Singapore and Penang. These were operational hubs for anti-piracy campaigns and provided them with secure anchorage for naval patrols. They also deployed more advanced naval technologies, including steam-powered warships that were faster and more effective than traditional sailing vessels. This technological superiority allowed the colonial navies to patrol and secure larger areas more efficiently.

The European colonial powers also forged alliances with the local rulers and communities, who suffered as much as anyone else from piracy. The Dutch East India Company engaged local Malay rulers and treaties to suppress piracy in the Strait of Malacca and its surrounding waters. Alliances like this were a huge part of gaining local support and intelligence that was needed for effective anti-piracy operations.

Along with these local alliances, European powers came together and coordinated military campaigns against pirate strongholds. The British undertook several punitive expeditions against pirate bases in Borneo and the Malay Archipelago. These were designed to dismantle pirate networks and established colonial control over some of the more key maritime routes.

The reduction of piracy led to more secure and stable trade routes. Now that the region was more secure, its economic development thrived. Merchants and traders could operate with greater confidence, leading to increased commercial activity and prosperity under colonial rule, as bad as colonial rule was.

By suppressing piracy, the colonial powers consolidated their control over Southeast Asia. The established colonial administrations now provided a framework for governance, law, and order that further stabilized the region.

The decline of piracy marked a shift in regional power dynamics. Where local pirate leaders once wielded considerable influence, colonial administrators took control. This diminished the traditional maritime power structures and incorporated Southeast Asia more firmly into the colonial empires of Europe.

Chapter 10 – Modern Piracy

Despite the decline of piracy, it was a major force on the seas by the mid-eighteenth century and never completely disappeared. Piracy very easily and quickly adapted to new environments and technologies. In the nineteenth and early twentieth centuries, it experienced a resurgence in certain regions. It still thrived in the South China Sea and parts of the Caribbean. This was often driven by local conflicts and economic hardships rather than the desire for wealth and easy access to it.

Decolonization after World War II led to political instability in a lot of areas, and this type of instability creates an environment that supports piracy. Piracy in modern times has been concentrated in several key regions, and each has its unique challenges and characteristics.

Gulf of Aden

The Gulf of Aden, situated between Yemen and Somalia, became a piracy hot spot in the early 2000s due to the collapse of the Somali government in 1991. When the government collapsed, there was widespread lawlessness and economic despair. Local fishermen faced the intrusion of foreign vessels into their fishing waters and began to hijack ships as a form of self-defense. These initial acts of passion slowly turned into a more organized and lucrative criminal enterprise and became increasingly more profitable. Pirates started to target large commercial vessels and demanded substantial ransoms that often averaged around $1 million per hijacked ship.

The international community launched several programs to combat piracy in the Gulf of Aden. The largest among these was the European Union's Operation Atalanta, initiated in 2008. NATO also contributed to the efforts with Operation Ocean Shield, and the United States led Combined Task Force 151. All these efforts involved patrolling the waters, escorting commercial ships, and conducting anti-piracy missions. By 2012, these efforts had significantly reduced the number of successful pirate attacks in the gulf.

Occasional attacks still occur because of the ongoing regional instability. A perfect example of this was the successful hijacking of the Aris 13 oil tanker in 2017. However, this was the first incident in five years. Completely eradicating piracy in this area is an incredible challenge. Factors like drought, famine, and frustration over illegal fishing by foreign vessels continue to drive individuals in this area toward piracy simply as a means of economic survival.

The Gulf of Aden is a critical maritime route. Over 20,000 ships, including a significant portion of the global oil trade, travel through annually. International trade and economic stability requires security in these shipping routes. The persistence of piracy in this region underscores the need for ongoing vigilance and cooperation among naval forces worldwide, something that has continued since the Golden Age of Piracy.

The Strait of Malacca

The Strait of Malacca, which connects the Indian Ocean with the South China Sea, has been a key maritime route for centuries. It's so important because it's the passageway for approximately 40 percent of the world's trade. This makes it a prime target for piracy. The narrowness of the strait and the high volume of traffic make it even more vulnerable.

Modern piracy in the Strait of Malacca involves three categories: opportunistic criminals seeking easy profit, organized crime syndicates, and groups with political or terrorist motivations. The pirates here often engage in armed robberies and hijackings. They target ships for their valuable cargo or simply for ransom. The pirate strategies are getting highly sophisticated. They use advanced technologies like GPS and automatic weapons, which has increased the complexity of fighting these threats.

Regional cooperation in the area has intensified to fight the high incidence of piracy. Indonesia, Malaysia, Singapore, and Thailand have all worked together through initiatives like the Malacca Straits Patrols to enhance maritime security. They've created coordinated naval patrols, information sharing, and joint exercises to help deter pirate activities.

Incidents of piracy have significantly diminished over the years thanks to the increased presence of naval forces and the implementation of security protocols. Still, they remain a concern. From January to March 2023, there were twenty-five reported incidents of armed robbery against ships in the strait. This was a 9 percent increase from the previous year. Fighting piracy in the Strait of Malacca is an ongoing challenge, and completely eradicating it seems to be nearly impossible. This is because economic disparities, corruption, and the involvement of local criminal elements drive people to piracy on a regular basis.

The Strait of Malacca is strategically significant and has drawn attention from major international powers. The United States, Japan, and China have all increased their naval presence in the region as part of a measure to safeguard their own economic interests. However, this international involvement can lead to geopolitical tensions because of more broad regional disputes.

Gulf of Guinea

The Gulf of Guinea is off the coast of West Africa and has become one of the most dangerous regions for maritime piracy. This area is plagued by piracy, armed robbery, and kidnapping. All of these have significant economic impacts and pose severe security threats to maritime businesses.

The pirates in this area are notorious for their violent attacks, which include kidnapping crew members for ransom and hijacking oil tankers. These pirates are well organized and heavily armed, making their attacks particularly dangerous. Recently, piracy incidents have been on the rise, with a concerning number of crew kidnappings and hijackings. In the first nine months of 2023, there were twenty-one reported incidents of piracy and armed robbery. These resulted in fourteen crew members being kidnapped and multiple instances of crews being taken hostage.

The shipping industry in the Gulf of Guinea suffers significant financial losses due to increased insurance premiums, security measures, and ransom payments. The disruption to trade routes affects the broader economy of the region and impacts the livelihoods of many who depend on maritime trade.

Efforts are being made to combat piracy in the Gulf of Guinea. These include the usual increased naval patrols by regional and international forces. With regional cooperation like the Yaoundé Architecture for Maritime Security, efforts are being made to enhance coordination and the response to piracy threats. These efforts are regularly challenged by weak law enforcement, corruption, and political instability.

Caribbean

Piracy in the Caribbean is far less notorious today than it was during its golden age. However, the region still experiences sporadic attacks. Modern piracy in the Caribbean usually involves smaller-scale operations that are carried out by fishermen and local criminals. Unlike piracy in the golden age, it's no longer about fighting back against a strict, hierarchical society. Most turned to piracy because of economic hardships.

The waters off Venezuela, Trinidad and Tobago, Guyana, and Suriname are particularly affected by piracy. The pirates in these areas often target anchored yachts and commercial fishing vessels. They rob them and then hold their crew members for ransom.

The severe economic crisis in Venezuela has forced many Venezuelan fishermen to turn to piracy to survive. They frequently attack vessels in the Gulf of Paria, which is a narrow strait of water between Venezuela and Trinidad and Tobago. There, they engage in smuggling and violent robberies.

As always, efforts are being made to combat the piracy that continues in the Caribbean. This includes increased patrols by regional navies and cooperation with international partners. Many of the Caribbean nations have limited resources, though, and rely on support from countries like the United States. For example, the US Coast Guard plays a critical role in providing maritime security assistance in the Caribbean.

Even with these efforts, piracy continues due to the ongoing economic challenges and complex geography in the region, which lacks comprehensive maritime security infrastructure. Inter-state tensions also contribute to the difficulties of addressing piracy.

Piracy here is driven by socioeconomic issues, and they are deeply rooted. High levels of poverty, unemployment, and political instability create an environment where piracy thrives. Pirates not only attack vessels but also engage in smuggling operations, moving contraband like drugs, weapons, and even basic necessities like food and diapers between Venezuela and neighboring countries.

While modern piracy in the Caribbean is less prominent than other regions like the Gulf of Guinea or the Strait of Malacca, it remains a significant threat.

International Responses to Modern Piracy

Starting in the Golden Age of Piracy, international efforts to combat piracy have been extensive. They continue to involve naval patrols, coordinated military exercises, and the implementation of anti-piracy legislation. The global economy means it's in everyone's best interest to safeguard maritime routes, protect vessels and crews, and address the root causes of piracy.

Naval Patrols and Operations

One of the most significant international responses has been the deployment of naval forces to patrol high-risk areas. The key operations include:

- **Combined Task Force 151 (CTF-151).** Established in 2009, CTF-151 is a multinational task force that focuses specifically on combating piracy in the Gulf of Aden and off the coast of Somalia. The force involves navies from various countries that work together to conduct patrols, escort ships, and respond to pirate attacks. They conducted the rescue operations during the *Maersk Alabama* hijacking incident.

- **Operation Atalanta.** As mentioned earlier, Operation Atlanta was launched by the European Union naval force in 2008. It was designed to protect vessels and deter piracy in the Somali Basin and the Indian Ocean. It's been instrumental in reducing piracy incidents because of its continuous maritime patrols and provision of escorts for World Food Programme shipments.

- **Obangame Express and Grand African NEMO.** These are annual multinational exercises that involve countries from the Gulf of Guinea and other international partners. Their focus is to improve regional cooperation, maritime security, and response capabilities to combat piracy, illegal fishing, and other threats.

Anti-Piracy Legislation

Countries continue to create legal frameworks to prosecute pirates and deter future incidents. The legalities have changed from the Golden Age of Piracy and are slightly less gruesome but still effectual. Key legislative efforts include the following:

- **The Yaoundé Code of Conduct.** Signed in 2013 by West and Central African countries, this legal framework aims to enforce maritime security using cooperation and information sharing. It has already led to the establishment of multinational maritime coordination centers and the development of regional maritime security strategies.

- **National Legislation.** Countries like Nigeria and Togo have created specific laws to criminalize piracy and armed robbery at sea. Nigeria's Suppression of Piracy and Other Maritime Offenses Act (SPOMO) of 2019 provides the nation with a new legal basis for prosecuting pirates and has resulted in several successful convictions.

Regional and International Cooperation

As European powers discovered in the seventeenth and eighteenth century, organizing internationally and creating regional bodies that cooperate is a critical part of combating piracy. This still applies today. Some modern examples include the following:

- **International Maritime Organization (IMO).** The IMO created a framework for international cooperation regarding maritime security. It has developed guidelines in best practices to enhance ship and port facility security.

- **United Nations Office on Drugs and Crime (UNODC).** The UNODC provides support for countries in development, especially with their legal frameworks. They help build law enforcement capacities and improve maritime domain awareness. They also facilitate regional cooperation and information sharing.

- **G7++ Friends of the Gulf of Guinea.** This group supports the implementation of the Yaoundé Code of Conduct. It also provides technical assistance, capacity building, and funding to the growth of maritime security in the Gulf of Guinea.

How Modern Piracy Differs from Historical Piracy

The fundamental nature of piracy as a criminal activity targeting maritime trade remains consistent. However, the methods, motivations, and responses have evolved dramatically.

The tactics and operations of modern piracy are significantly different from those of historical pirates. This is mostly reflected in changes in technology, economic conditions, and geopolitical situations. Historical pirates, if you recall, operated using sailing ships that were equipped with cannons and muskets. These vessels required extensive nautical skills for navigation and combat. The pirate crews often ranged from twenty to fifty men or women to manage the complex operations of their ships and execute their daring attacks on merchant vessels and coastal settlements.

In contrast, you do not have to be a sailor to be successful as a pirate today. Modern pirates use GPS and radar to help them track and intercept ships with greater precision. They don't have to rely on navigational skills and maritime knowledge as historical pirates did. They use speed boats and are armed with automatic weapons like AK-47s and rocket-propelled grenades. This allows for very swift and violent attacks. They often target smaller vessels because they're easier to board and hijack.

The motivations behind piracy have also changed. Historical pirates were motivated by a combination of economic gain, rebellion against oppressive maritime laws, and the pursuit of freedom. They operated in a context where state navies were relatively weak and the colonial trade routes were prosperous. There were ample opportunities for plunder. Modern piracy is largely driven by economic hardship and political instability.

Conclusion

Piracy is a world that is fascinating and tumultuous. You have now explored the evolution of piracy from ancient times to the present day. You've seen the various manifestations and impacts across several different historical periods.

Ancient civilizations like the Greeks, Romans, and Phoenicians saw their earliest instances of piracy on record, driven by the economic and political instability of the times. Moving into the medieval era, the Vikings dominated the northern seas. They brought a new era of fear and destruction to coastal settlements across Europe. This era also saw the first early maritime laws that were aimed at controlling these types of piracy. Medieval pirates like Eustace the Monk continued to demonstrate how piracy and mercenary activities blended together.

The Age of Exploration brought new technology and new opportunities for piracy. Piracy now expanded into the new world with all its gold and silver and riches. European colonial expansion fueled the rise of pirates, who preyed on treasure-laden ships that were returning from the colonies of the Americas. Notorious figures like Sir Francis Drake and Grace O'Malley became prominent pirates during an era where their exploits intertwined with national rivalries and colonial ambitions.

Piracy reached its golden age from the late seventeenth to the early eighteenth centuries. Pirates like Blackbeard and Bartholomew Roberts terrorized the Caribbean, the American coast, and the Indian Ocean. Piracy was an attractive way of life. These people banded together, establishing homes in pirate havens and creating a unique, diplomatic, and progressive culture for themselves. They created their own code of conduct and democratic practices within their crews to keep everything equal and fight against a system that viewed them as less than those around them.

We looked at the decline of piracy. Governments started making more concerted efforts to combat piracy, which, combined with the advances in naval technology, made piracy more difficult. Despite these efforts, the Barbary corsairs of the Mediterranean and the piracy in the Indian Ocean and Southeast Asia were a persistent threat. Even though piracy in the Caribbean fell, it did not find an end, simply a new beginning.

Piracy remains a significant issue in new regions. Modern pirates use advanced technology and operate in a globalized world. While international responses remain very similar to the past, including naval patrols and anti-piracy legislation, there are also efforts to fight the underlying causes that lead to piracy in the first place.

Piracy has left a lasting imprint on modern society, culture, and law. The image of pirates has been grossly romanticized and perpetuated by literature and popular media. This romantic version of piracy contrasts starkly with its historical brutality. Pirates were brutal, violent criminals, but the appeal is in the way they lived their lives. What's romanticized is their decision to fight against the status quo, against a harsh and divided society. The Pirates of the Golden Age were the epitome of rebels fighting against a government that fought them at every turn as they sought success and a better life. These depictions have cemented pirates as cultural icons. They became symbols of rebellion and adventure.

Legally, the struggle against piracy shaped maritime law, influenced frameworks like the United Nations Convention on the Law of the Sea (UNCLOS) and created more international cooperation needed to safeguard maritime routes.

Piracy will continue to evolve. Technology is constantly advancing, and global economic activity is shifting. Cyber piracy emerges as a new frontier, with hackers targeting maritime operations through digital means. Global trade continues to expand, and the fight against piracy requires more innovative strategies to cope. It's important to focus on addressing the underlying socioeconomic factors that draw individuals to a life of piracy.

If you enjoyed this book, a review on Amazon would be greatly appreciated because it would mean a lot to hear from you.

To leave a review:

1. Open your camera app.
2. Point your mobile device at the QR code.
3. The review page will appear in your web browser.

Thanks for your support!

Here's another book by Captivating History that you might like

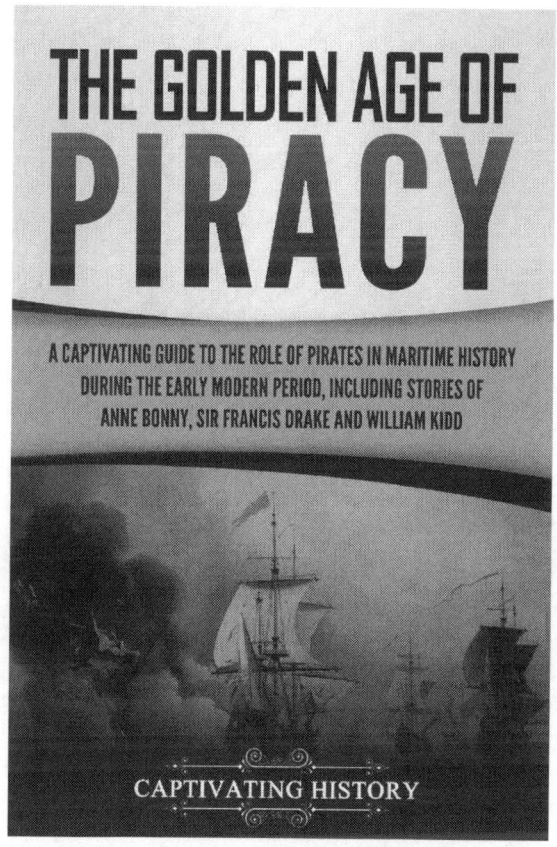

Free Bonus from Captivating History (Available for a Limited time)

Hi History Lovers!

Now you have a chance to join our exclusive history list so you can get your first history ebook for free as well as discounts and a potential to get more history books for free!

Simply visit the link below to join.

Or, Scan the QR code!

captivatinghistory.com/ebook

Also, make sure to follow us on Facebook, X, and YouTube by searching for Captivating History.

Resources

Chapter 1

Britannica, T. Editors of Encyclopedia. "The Time Julius Caesar Was Captured by Pirates." *Encyclopedia Brittanica*, January 25, 2019. https://www.britannica.com/story/the-time-julius-caesar-was-captured-by-pirates.

Macquire, Kelly. "History of the Phoenicians: The Maritime Superpowers of the Mediterranean." World History Encyclopedia, November 14, 2021. https://www.worldhistory.org/video/2680/history-of-the-phoenicians-the-maritime-superpower/.

Mark, Joshua J. "Pirates in the Ancient Mediterranean." World History Encyclopedia, August 19, 2019. https://www.worldhistory.org/Piracy/.

Mark, Joshua J. "Pirates of the Mediterranean." World History Encyclopedia, August 23, 2019. https://www.worldhistory.org/article/47/pirates-of-the-mediterranean/.

Mingren, Woo. "Piracy in the Ancient Mediterranean and the Notorious Cilicians." Ancient Origins, February 19, 2024. https://www.ancient-origins.net/history-famous-people/cilician-pirates-007309.

"Piracy in Ancient Greece." *Ancient Blogger* (blog). https://ancientblogger.com/piracy-in-ancient-greece-episode-notes/. Accessed June 12, 2024.

"Piracy in Ancient Greece: 8 Famous Ancient Greek Pirates." Greece High Definition, July 28, 2022. https://www.greecehighdefinition.com/blog/piracy-in-ancient-greece-famous-ancient-greek-pirates. Accessed June 12, 2024.

Quinn, Josephine. "All at sea: The maritime lives of the ancient Phoenicians." Princeton University Press, June 23, 2020. https://press.princeton.edu/ideas/all-at-sea-the-maritime-lives-of-the-ancient-phoenicians.

Chapter 2

Ferrer, Maria Teresa. "Catalan Commerce in the late Middle Ages." From *Catalon Historical Review 5* (2012). https://www.medievalists.net/2017/09/catalan-commerce-late-middle-ages/.

Goodyear, Michael. "The Medieval Pirates' Nest of Crete." Medevialists.net, https://www.medievalists.net/2021/12/the-medieval-pirates-nest-of-crete/. Accessed June 14, 2024.

Groeneveld, Emma. "Viking Warfare." World History Encyclopedia, June 01, 2018. https://www.worldhistory.org/Viking_Warfare/.

Jaspert, N. "'Piracy,' Connectivity and Seaborne Power in the Middle Ages. In C. Buchet & M. Balard (Eds.), *The Sea in History - The Medieval World.* Boydell & Brewer, 2017.

Mark, Joshua J. "Viking Raids in Britain." World History Encyclopedia, March 20, 2018. https://www.worldhistory.org/article/1197/viking-raids-in-britain/.

Martinez, J. "Lindisfarne Raid." *Encyclopedia Britannica,* June 1, 2024. https://www.britannica.com/event/Lindisfarne-Raid.

Mingren, Wu. "Eustace the Monk: Talented Pirate for the French and the English." Ancient Origins, last updated December 14, 2020. https://www.ancient-origins.net/history-famous-people/eustace-monk-0014670.

Schoppert, Stephanie. "A Pirate's Life: 6 Swashbuckling Medieval Pirates." History Collection, June 20, 2017. https://historycollection.com/pirates-life-6-swashbuckling-medieval-pirates/.

Wilczynski, Krzysztof. "Impact of Piracy on International Laws and Treaties." *Pirates! Fact and Legend* (blog). https://www.piratesinfo.com/history-of-piracy/impact-and-influence-of-piracy/impact-of-piracy-on-international-laws-and-treaties/. Accessed June 14, 2024.

Wilczynski, Krzysztof. "Middle Age Pirates: Sea Raiders and Plunderers." *Pirates! Fact and Legend* (blog). https://www.piratesinfo.com/history-of-piracy/ancient-piracy-antiquity-to-middle-ages/middle-age-pirates-sea-raiders-and-plunderers/. Accessed June 14, 2024.

Chapter 3

Jaspert, N. "'Piracy,' connectivity and seaborne power in the Middle Ages. In C. Buchet & M. Balard (Eds.), *The Sea in History - The Medieval World.* Boydell & Brewer, 2017.

Cartwright, Mark. "Spanish Treasure Fleets." World History Encyclopedia, November 10, 2021. https://www.worldhistory.org/Spanish_Treasure_Fleets/.

Britannica, T. Editors of Encyclopedia. "Spanish Treasure Fleet." *Encyclopedia Britannica*, February 14, 2011. https://www.britannica.com/topic/Spanish-treasure-fleet.

History.com Editors. "Sir Francis Drake." A&E Television Networks, updated June 6, 2023. https://www.history.com/topics/exploration/sir-francis-drake.

Alchin, Linda. "The Age of Exploration." Elizabethan Era. https://www.elizabethan-era.org.uk/the-age-of-exploration.htm Accessed June 16, 2024.

Wilczynski, Krzysztof. "Famous Pirates." *Pirates! Fact and Legend* (blog). https://www.piratesinfo.com/famous-pirates/. Accessed June 16, 2024.

Walser, Mike. "Piracy and America." *Pirates! Fact and Legend* (blog). https://www.piratesinfo.com/history-of-piracy/golden-age-of-piracy/piracy-and-america/ Accessed June 16, 2024.

"The Victual Brothers." Military Wiki. https://military-history.fandom.com/wiki/Victual_Brothers. Accessed June 16, 2024.

Sheppard, Simon and Schaitberger, Linda. "Bei Störtebekers Bart!" Revisionist.net. https://www.revisionist.net/likedeelers.html Accessed June 16, 2024.

Chapter 4

Aya, Radwan. "The Golden Age of Piracy: Unveiling the Caribbean's Historical Saga and Myths." *Connolly Cove* (blog), last updated March 15, 2024. https://www.connollycove.com/the-golden-age-of-piracy-caribbean-history/.

Cartwright, Mark. "Golden Age of Piracy." Word History Encyclopedia, October 12, 2021. https://www.worldhistory.org/Golden_Age_of_Piracy/.

Milligan, Mark. "Tortuga – The Pirate Stronghold." Heritage Daily, December 30, 2020. https://www.heritagedaily.com/2020/12/tortuga-the-pirate-stronghold/136613.

Mitchell, Robbie. "Pirate Havens: 8 of the Most Notorious Pirate Strongholds." Ancient Origins, updated April 2, 2023. https://www.ancient-origins.net/ancient-places-americas/pirate-strongholds-0018178.

Pullman, Michael. "Madagascar: A Pirate's Paradise." Wild Frontiers Adventure Travel, April 19, 2017. https://www.wildfrontierstravel.com/en_US/blog/madagascar-a-pirate-s-paradise.

Rule, Chris. "Madagascar's Piratical Past." *Pirates! Fact and Legend* (blog). https://www.piratesinfo.com/pirate-facts-and-pirate-legends/pirate-strongholds-hideouts/piratical-history-of-madagascar/ Accessed June 18, 2024.

Taylor, Katie. "The Pirates of Madagascar." Travel Local, May 15, 2018. https://www.travellocal.com/en/articles/the-pirates-of-madagascar.

"The Golden Age of Piracy." Royal Museums Greenwich. https://www.rmg.co.uk/stories/topics/golden-age-piracy. Accessed June 18, 2024.

"The Golden Age of Piracy: Brethren of the Coast at Tortuga." Golden Age of Piracy. https://goldenageofpiracy.org/history/pirate-governments/brethren-of-the-coast-at-tortuga Accessed June 18, 2024.

"The Golden Age of Piracy: Nassau." Golden Age of Piracy. https://goldenageofpiracy.org/locations/nassau. Accessed June 18, 2024.

Chapter 5

Andrews, Evan. "The Most Successful Pirate You've Never Heard Of." A&E Television Networks, updated August 31, 2018. https://www.history.com/news/henry-everys-bloody-pirate-raid-320-years-ago.

"Anne Bonny, Pirate." National Park Service, updated May 17, 2019. https://www.nps.gov/people/anne-bonny-pirate.htm.

"Calico Jack." Crime Museum. https://www.crimemuseum.org/crime-library/international-crimes/calico-jack/. Accessed June 18, 2024.

Cartwright, Mark. "Anne Bonny." World History Encyclopedia, August 23, 2021. https://www.worldhistory.org/Anne_Bonny/.

Cartwright, Mark. "Blackbeard." World History Encyclopedia, August 19, 2021. https://www.worldhistory.org/Blackbeard/.

Cartwright, Mark. "Henry Every." World History Encyclopedia, September 15, 2021. https://www.worldhistory.org/Henry_Every/.

Cartwright, Mark. "Henry Morgan." World History Encyclopedia, October 25, 2021. https://www.worldhistory.org/Henry_Morgan/.

"Charles Vane." Golden Age of Piracy. https://goldenageofpiracy.org/pirates/flying-gang/charles-vane. Accessed June 18, 2024.

Codlin, Robin. "Mary Read, Pirate." Historic UK. https://www.historic-uk.com/HistoryUK/HistoryofEngland/Mary-Read-Pirate. Accessed June 18, 2024.

Crawford, Amy. "The Gentleman Pirate." *Smithsonian Magazine*, July 31, 2007. https://www.smithsonianmag.com/history/the-gentleman-pirate-159418520/.

Fraga, Kaleena. "The Story of Anne Bonny, The Sword-Wielding Pirate Who Ruled The Caribbean." All That's Interesting, updated March 17, 2024. https://allthatsinteresting.com/anne-bonny.

Johnson, Ben. "Captain William Kidd." Historic UK. https://www.historic-uk.com/HistoryUK/HistoryofScotland/Captain-William-Kidd/. Accessed June 18, 2024.

Lewis, Jone Johnson. "A Profile of Notorious Female Pirate, Mary Read." ThoughtCo, updated July 03, 2019. https://www.thoughtco.com/mary-read-a-profile-of-the-notorious-female-pirate-4158297.

Minster, Christopher. "Biography of Captain Henry Morgan, Welsh Privateer." ThoughtCo, updated June 5, 2019. https://www.thoughtco.com/captain-morgan-greatest-of-the-privateers-2136378.

Minster, Christopher. "Biography of Captain William Kidd, Scottish Pirate." ThoughtCo, updated May 08, 2019. https://www.thoughtco.com/captain-william-kidd-2136225.

Minster, Christopher. "Biography of Charles Vane, English Pirate." ThoughtCo, updated July 21, 2019. https://www.thoughtco.com/biography-of-charles-vane-2136363.

Minster, Christopher. "Biography of Edward 'Blackbeard' Teach, Pirate." ThoughtCo, updated July 15, 2019. https://www.thoughtco.com/biography-of-edward-blackbeard-teach-2136364.

Minster, Christopher. "Biography of John 'Calico Jack' Rackham, Famed Pirate." ThoughtCo, updated May 15, 2019. https://www.thoughtco.com/biography-of-john-calico-jack-rackham-2136377.

Minster, Christopher. "Biography of Stede Bonnet, the Gentleman Pirate." ThoughtCo, January 03, 2020. https://www.thoughtco.com/stede-bonnet-the-gentleman-pirate-2136231.

"Thomas Tew." The Golden Age of Piracy, https://goldenageofpiracy.org/pirates/pirate-rounders/thomas-tew. Accessed June 18, 2024.

"Thomas Tew (unknown – 1695)." *History of Piracy* (blog). https://historyofpiracy.weebly.com/thomas-tew.html. Accessed June 18, 2024.

"Who was Blackbeard?" Royal Museums Greenwich. https://www.rmg.co.uk/stories/topics/blackbeard-edward-teach-pirate. Accessed June 18, 2024.

Yost, Russel. "Henry Morgan Fact and Life." The History Junkie, updated November 3, 2023. https://thehistoryjunkie.com/henry-morgan-facts-and-life/.

Chapter 6

Britannica, T. Editors of Encyclopedia. "Fluyt: Dutch Ship." *Encyclopedia Britannica.* https://www.britannica.com/technology/fluyt. Accessed June 21, 2024.

Britannica, T. Editors of Encyclopedia. "Galleon." *Encyclopedia Britannica,* September 7, 2024. https://www.britannica.com/technology/galleon.

Cartwright, Mark. "Pirate Weapons in the Golden Age of Piracy." World History Encyclopedia, August 31, 2021. https://www.worldhistory.org/article/1825/pirate-weapons-in-the-golden-age-of-piracy/.

"Common Tactics on How Pirates Took Merchant Ships." *Pirates Ahoy! Uniting Maritime Enthusiasts* (blog), updated December 5, 2021.

https://www.piratesahoy.net/wiki/ship-capturing-techniques/.

"Fluyt (16th-18th Century)."Deutsches Historisches Museum. https://www.dhm.de/mediathek/en/ship-types/milestones-in-the-history-of-european-shipbuilding/09-fluyt/. Accessed June 21, 2024.

"Pirate Ships: An In-Depth Look at Their Types and History." Republic of Pirates. https://republicofpirates.net/pirate-ships-an-in-depth-look-at-their-types-and-history/ Accessed June 21, 2024.

"Pirate Ships: Brigantine." Golden Age of Piracy. https://goldenageofpiracy.org/pirate-ships/pirate-ship-types/brigantine. Accessed June 21, 2024.

"Pirate Ships: Frigate." The Golden Age of Piracy. https://goldenageofpiracy.org/pirate-ships/pirate-ship-types/frigates. Accessed June 21, 2024.

"Pirate Ships: Schooner." Golden Age of Piracy. https://goldenageofpiracy.org/pirate-ships/pirate-ship-types/schooner. Accessed June 21, 2024.

"Pirate Ships: Sloop." Golden Age of Piracy. https://goldenageofpiracy.org/pirate-ships/pirate-ship-types/sloop. Accessed June 21, 2024.

"Schooner 101." *The Liberte* (blog), January 18, 2019. https://www.theliberte.com/blog/schooner-101-what-do-you-know-about-the-schooner/.

"The History of the Brigantine." Venture Sail Holidays. https://venturesailholidays.com/history-of-the-brigantine/. Accessed June 21, 2024.

"The History of Pirate Ships: From Galleons to Sloops." Sunshine Scenic Tours, April 14, 2023. https://boattoursjohnspass.com/the-history-of-pirate-ships-from-galleons-to-sloops/.

Vallar, Cindy. "Pirate Tactics." *Pirates & Privateers: The History of Maritime Piracy* (blog), http://www.cindyvallar.com/tactics.html. Accessed June 21, 2024.

Chapter 7

Drymalski, Noah. "Pirate Code of Conduct in the 1700s (Founders of Democracy)." *The History Junkie* (blog), November 28, 2023. https://thehistoryjunkie.com/pirate-code-of-conduct/.

Fraga, Kaleena."Inside the Blood-Soaked Story of the Jolly Roger Pirate Flag." All Things Interesting, August 23, 2022. https://allthatsinteresting.com/jolly-roger-flag.

Irvine, Amy. "The Pirates' Code: Laws and Life Aboard Ship." History Hit, April 28, 2023. https://www.historyhit.com/the-pirates-code-laws-and-life-aboard-ship/.

"The Pirate Code." The Golden Age of Piracy. https://goldenageofpiracy.org/culture/pirate-code. Accessed June 23, 2024.

Wilczynki, Krzysztof. "Pirate Legends, Life & Culture." *Pirates! Fact and Legend* (blog). https://www.piratesinfo.com/pirate-facts-and-pirate-legends/. Accessed June 23, 2024.

Wilczynki, Krzysztof. "The Dubious Art of Pirate Injury Compensation." *Pirates! Fact and Legend* (blog). https://www.piratesinfo.com/pirate-facts-and-pirate-legends/a-pirates-life-for-me/pirate-injury-compensation-dubious-deals/. Accessed June 23, 2024.

Chapter 8

Butler, Nic. "The Pirate Executions of 1718." Charleston County Public Library, December 8, 2018. https://www.ccpl.org/charleston-time-machine/pirate-executions-1718.

Minster, Christopher. "The Golden Age of Piracy: Blackbeard, Bart Roberts, Jack Rackham, and More." ThoughtCo, January 6, 2020. https://www.thoughtco.com/the-golden-age-of-piracy-2136277.

"Pirate Hunters." The Golden Age of Piracy. https://goldenageofpiracy.org/history/pirate-hunters. Accessed June 25, 2024.

"Pirates: The Royal Navy and the Suppression of Maritime Raiding 1620-1830." *Military History Matters*, April 27, 2012. https://www.military-history.org/feature/17th-century/pirates-the-royal-navy-and-the-suppression-of-maritime-raiding-1620-1830.htm.

"The Golden Age of Piracy." Royal Museums Greenwich. https://www.rmg.co.uk/stories/topics/golden-age-piracy. Accessed June 25, 2024.

Chapter 9

Amirell, S. E. "Maritime Piracy and Raiding in Southeast Asia: Local and Global Perspectives." In *Globalization and its Counterforces in Southeast Asia*, edited by Terence Chong. ISEAS–Yusof Ishak Institute, 2008.

"Aruj Barbarossa: Most Notorious Pirate of the Barbary Corsairs." Ancient Origins, updated August 9, 2016. https://www.ancient-origins.net/history-famous-people/aruj-barbarossa-most-notorious-pirate-barbary-corsairs-006416.

"Barbarossa Brothers, Barbary Pirates." Pirates Realm. https://www.thepiratesrealm.com/Barbarossa%20Brothers.html. Accessed June 27, 2024.

Capp, Bernard. "Introduction." In *British Slaves and Barbary Corsairs, 1580-1750*. Oxford, 2022; online ed. Oxford Academic, April 21, 2022.

Colás, Alejandro. "Barbary Coast in the Expansion of International Society: Piracy, Privateering, and Corsairing as Primary Institutions." *Review of International Studies* 42, no. 5 (2016): 840–857.

https://doi.org/10.1017/S0260210516000152.

Cartwright, Mark. "Zheng Yi Sao." World History Encyclopedia, November 15, 2021. https://www.worldhistory.org/Zheng_Yi_Sao/.

Jamieson, Alan. *Lords of the Sea: A History of the Barbary Corsairs*. Reaktion Books: 2012.

Mohamed, Fatma. "History's Most Successful Female Pirate Queen: Zheng Yi Sao." *Connolly Cove* (blog), May 5, 2024. https://www.connollycove.com/pirate-queen/ Accessed: June 27, 2024.

Nathan, Joshua. "Zheng Yi Sao: The Powerful Woman that Became the Most Feared Pirate in History." Cultura Colectiva, September 19, 2023. https://culturacolectiva.com/en/history/zheng-yi-sao-female-pirate/.

Nichols, Adam. "Murad Reis – The Commander of the Sale Corsairs." *Corsairs & Captives* (blog), October 10, 2021. https://corsairsandcaptivesblog.com/murad-reis-the-commander-of-the-sale-corsairs/.

"Turgut Reis." The Way of the Pirates. http://www.thewayofthepirates.com/famous-pirates/turgut-reis/. Accessed June 27, 2024.

Chapter 10

Cooke, Jennifer G. "Piracy in the Gulf of Aden." Center for Strategic and International Studies, October 2, 2008. https://www.csis.org/analysis/piracy-gulf-aden.

"Fighting Piracy: Three Regions Your Navy Combats Piracy around the Globe." *All Hands: Magazine of the US Navy*. https://allhands.navy.mil/Features/Antipiracy/. Accessed June 29, 2024.

"IBM Piracy & Armed Robbery Map 2014." ICC Commercial Crime Services. https://www.icc-ccs.org/piracy-reporting-centre/live-piracy-map. Accessed June 29, 2024.

McKnight, Terry. "End Piracy in the Gulf of Aden." *Proceedings Today* 143 no. 6 (2017). https://www.usni.org/magazines/proceedings/2017/june/end-piracy-gulf-aden.

"Mid-year IMB Report Reveals Rise in Maritime Piracy and Armed Robbery." International Chamber of Commerce (ICC). https://iccwbo.org/news-publications/news/mid-year-imb-report-reveals-rise-in-maritime-piracy-and-armed-robbery/. Accessed June 29, 2024.

"Ongoing Decline in Gulf of Guinea's Piracy, Armed Robbery Encouraging, But Support Needed to Fully Implement Yaoundé Architecture, Briefers Tell Security Council." United Nations Media Coverage and Press Releases, June 21, 2023. https://press.un.org/en/2023/sc15331.doc.htm.

"Piracy and Armed Robbery Against Ships: Jan – March 2023." ICC International Maritime Bureau. https://www.icc-ccs.org/reports/2023%20-%20Jan%20-%20Mar%20IMB%20Piracy%20and%20Armed%20Robbery%20Report.pdf. Accessed June 29, 2024.

"Piracy, Armed Robbery Declining in the Gulf of Guinea, But Enhanced National, Regional Efforts Needed for Stable Maritime Security, Top Official Tells Security Council." United Nations Media Coverage and Press Releases, November 22, 2022. https://press.un.org/en/2022/sc15113.doc.htm.

Venezuela Investigative Unit. "Pirates Control Ocean Between Venezuela, Trinidad and Tobago." Insight Crime, January 21, 2019. https://insightcrime.org/news/analysis/pirates-venezuela-trinidad-and-tobago/.

Venezuela Investigative Unit. "Report Highlights How Venezuela Crisis Fuels Piracy, Contraband in the Caribbean." Insight Crime, February 5, 2018. https://insightcrime.org/news/brief/report-highlights-venezuela-crisis-fuels-piracy-contraband-caribbean/.

Image Sources

[1] https://commons.wikimedia.org/wiki/File:Edward_Teach_Commonly_Call%27d_Black_Beard_(bw).jpg

[2] https://commons.wikimedia.org/wiki/File:Bonnet.gif

[3] https://commons.wikimedia.org/wiki/File:Niagara_(1895_sloop)_big_(cropped).png

[4] By dgenge. Free to use under Pixabay; https://pixabay.com/service/license-summary/; https://pixabay.com/vectors/schooner-boat-sailboat-yacht-8149048/

[5] https://commons.wikimedia.org/wiki/File:La-fregate-de-18-la-penelope-1802-1816-par-francois-roux-18772.jpg

[6] https://commons.wikimedia.org/wiki/File:Spanish_Galleon.jpg

[7] Karlsson, Anneli (color correction by Blockhaj), CC BY 4.0 <https://creativecommons.org/licenses/by/4.0>, via Wikimedia Commons; https://commons.wikimedia.org/wiki/File:%C3%85land_piratflagga_(color_fix).png

Printed in Dunstable, United Kingdom

70550794R00060